DISNEY'S

1 | WONDERFUL WORLD OF KNOWLEDGE

Disney's

Wonderful World of Knowledge

THE DANBURY PRESS

THE DANBURY PRESS

a division of Grolier Enterprises, Inc.

ROBERT B. CLARKE	*Publisher*
ROBERT G. BARTNER	*Marketing Director*
GILBERT EVANS	*Creative Director*
JACK JAGET	*Design*
THE STONEHOUSE PRESS	*Production Supervision*

"Disney's WONDERFUL WORLD OF KNOWLEDGE"
is an updated and enlarged English version of
an encyclopedia heretofore printed in the Italian language by
ARNOLDO MONDADORI EDITORE, MILAN
and entitled (in English Translation) "Disney ENCYCLOPEDIA"

CONTENTS

LIFE UNDER THE JUNGLE TREES

Hello, boys and girls. I'm your friend Donald Duck. Isn't it marvelous that the editors of this first volume of our encyclopedia have asked me to travel with you all over the world! Incredible, but true, and we are going together to meet the animals most representative of all on the planet: the mammals. Among all existing animals, mammals are those that have reached the highest level of development. All, or nearly all, of them have fur; almost all have four legs, except some which have only two, like bats, or have fins, like dolphins. Nearly all mammals give birth to their young alive—they don't lay eggs—and they nurse them. As you can see, being your guide is a very important job for me.

I really can't tell you why the authors have chosen me, though. Unless . . . Oh, now I remember. It all began, no doubt, when I was on my way home by way of Africa and found a lost, hungry and yowling leopard cub in my arms. It was quite an occasion, because I mistook the cub for a cat and took it home to meet Tabby. What a mistake! Tabby behaved very badly indeed and ran to the dog shelter for protection. So, of course, I had to take the cub back where I found him. Or he found me. In my opinion, that experience is why I was chosen to be your guide. Anyway, that's enough of an introduction. Let's get going. After you, naturally.

Just look: We can see an impenetrable green ocean stretching before us: the jungle. Thousands of miles, and millions of plants all intertwined and tangled around each other, above and below and around us. There are plants that try to survive in the shade of others that are stronger and more powerful. Over here are plants that try to overpower and conquer others by making room with the strength of their branches, to get the better of them in height and reaching, crown outspread towards the light and sun they need for life.

Jungles differ, according to the continent on which they are found, and so do their inhabitants. Let's start with a visit (just a quick one) to that vast band of permanent jungle surrounding the earth. It lies between the tropics and extends from South America to Central Africa, touches part of India and the Far East and reaches Northern Australia. My comments about this green jungle belt will be brief and I only mention it to explain why animals choose certain characteristics.

A jungle is a region, usually hot, with very thick, almost impenetrable vegetation, where intertwined branches form a roof that is sometimes 100 feet thick!

9

The animals that live there have a very developed ability to climb, jump and grip. They climb, they jump from branch to branch, they shimmy up and down the trunks of trees—with the skill of monkeys. And that is odd, for that is what most of them are!

These animals with this tremendous talent for climbing are the primates, mostly monkeys, but also you and me! The great Swedish botanist Linnaeus coined the name 'primate' as if to emphasize the superiority of this order of mammals over others. Of all the primates, and not all of them live in trees, the monkeys

The spider monkey is among the strangest of the jungle animals around the Amazon River basin in South America. Lively and chattering, this primate has very long arms and legs and an even longer prehensile tail—which means he can grasp with it, or wrap it around a trunk. If he were spread out flat, he would resemble a spider—hence his name. Spider monkeys are able to cross a river by forming a living chain. They hold each other by the tail and swing from tree top to tree top over water to reach the other side. The funny little face on the right belongs to the squirrel monkey. His tail is soft and warm, and an unusual 16 inches in length.

are best suited to the life of a climber. If we look at their paws, we see that their 'hands' have five fingers, and their 'feet' have toes, which actually look more like fingers. This helps them to grip objects. They can use their prehensile tails for this purpose also. Other animals have prehensile tails, among them the opossum, the kinkajou, many rodents, and most monkeys of the South American rain forests. It seems odd that the monkeys of South Africa and Asia do not have prehensile tails, while many other mammals, such as certain Australian tree-dwelling marsupials, some rats, the scaley anteater, the bearcat of Indochina do.

THE HOWLER MONKEYS

Boys and girls, there is something important I want to talk about before we continue. I just wish you had a chance to

hear the thousands and thousands of sounds in the jungle. At first glance, you would not think there was very much animal life in the tropical forest because there would be nothing you could see moving in all that luxurious vegetation. Part of the reason is that the animals hide, especially during the day, among leaves and tree trunks, in tree top and under-

(*opposite, top*) *This beautiful yellow-chested creature is of the cercopithecus species. He is found throughout Africa, in wooded areas near rivers and streams. (opposite, bottom) This is the chimpanzee, who is intelligent and the only animal capable of using tools, even though they are primitive ones. He uses sticks to pry out termites and worms, and picks leaves from which to drink.*

On this page is the orangutan, who, up in a tree, acts like Tarzan. It is another matter when he is on the ground, for his legs are short and quite weak. His name in Malay means 'man of the forest,' and he is most often found on the islands of Borneo and Sumatra. (below) Here is a cercopithecus 'neglectus' with sideburns and a white beard.

brush. Much has been written about the silence of the jungle during the daytime as though daylight were something obnoxious and oppressive. There might be a shrill scream of a bird to break the silence, the momentary chatter of a squirrel, the droning flight of an insect perhaps, the cataclysmic crash of a giant tree falling, or the burbling of a nearby river. Otherwise silence. But it is at night that the animal world comes to life, as if by magic or the wave of an invisible baton, the deafening orchestration of a jungle concert opens up. The locust with their metallic clamor, the croaking of the tree frogs, the shrill screaming of thousands of parrots preparing to sleep, and the tormented shrieks of the howler monkeys—all join the chorus.

These howler monkeys are found primarily in South America. That is, they are found in the trees of South America, for they rarely leave their tree top, even for a drink—the howler monkey quenches his thirst by licking damp leaves. It is easy to understand why he is called a howler

13

monkey. His shriek is as loud as the roar of a lion, and can be heard a half-mile away. Can you imagine a troop of thirty or forty howler monkeys in full voice? The effect is similar to a very modern opera. These monkeys live together in groups and can defend themselves when danger threatens by howling. The noise is absolutely terrifying.

But in spite of all this, when I see a baby howler monkey, my heart melts. When they are just born, the little ones hug their mother's breast. For a full year after this they ride her back, like a papoose. After this year, the little monkey takes his first steps along the branches of the giant trees. It is now that he becomes brave, even foolhardy. For he knows that if he falls, the whole troop, all of his aunts, uncles and cousins, will rush to his aid. All howling, naturally.

At nightfall it is as though the jungle is bewitched, for it is now that the jaguars and the leopards begin to roar. Later on, in dead of night, only a chorus of tree frogs and insects remind us that the jungle

The pigmy anteater on this page wouldn't leave his home —that is, his branch— for all the ants in the world. He lives, sleeps, drinks, and rears his young without ever leaving his home branch. He inhabits the South American jungle. (opposite, p. 14) The howler monkey is equipped with an unusual sound box in his throat and this amplifies his voice to scare his enemies.

is really alive, whether we hear it or not. And then towards dawn, there is a new round of sounds: it is the early risers going in search of food and drink. And then once more in the fullness of day the jungle is quiet.

That's right, boys and girls. During the day we could walk in the jungle for hours without seeing even the shadow of the mammals we are seeking. If we take a more careful look, however, we can see the fresh print of a paw on the ground. The most visible tracks in the African jungle are those left by the wart hog and other wild pigs that follow elephant trails and feed on roots and fallen leaves. You'll also find the tracks of the baboon who follows the wart hog, to scavenge his leftovers, and to find the worms and scorpions unearthed in the tracks. Picture yourself in the very heart of a jungle or equatorial rain forest. Above your head is a never-ending green roof made of the intertwined branches and leaves of trees— so thick that almost no light penetrates. The air will seem still to you, and it is, because the wind, like the light, barely penetrates. This is why the depths of a rain forest is almost always completely still. This stillness is vital for the smallest of the creatures who live in the forest.

Because of the lack of any breeze to carry scents, many mammals of the jungle have little use for their sense of smell, or for their sense of sight because of the darkness. In this, they are unlike the animals which live in open spaces. The okapi which lives in the jungles of the Congo is relatively blind, compared with the antelopes which live on the prairies of the same region. The hearing of the okapi, however, is very highly developed. This is also why the tree monkeys scream in the way they do—to keep in touch with each other.

But let us move on. It is easy to see that the denseness of vegetation in the jungle makes it hard for animals to move swiftly on the ground. For this reason, the larger mammals are at a disadvantage; but this disadvantage is only relative, because the elephant, the buffalo, the leopard, and other large mammals can bat down their victim with one stretch of a heavy paw, and too bad for him. Other mammals live in these jungles, including small quadrupeds with a limited horn development. In fact, still in Africa, the jungle antelopes are small, with short horns—such as the bongo and the trageladeer—the pudu which is only 15½ inches at the shoulder.

15

Here are the eyes of a tiger, a puma and
an African lynx—although the lynx seems to
have his closed! They are three beautiful,
fierce and unapproachable animals. At one and
a half months of age, the tiger cub learns
his first hunting lore. At about two, he
leaves his 'parents' home to lead his own
independent life in the jungles of Asia. The
puma purrs as he breathes in and out and
sounds like a contented house cat, to whom he
is a distant relation. He hunts at night and
is the terror of the monkeys. A caracal, or
African lynx, is the most elegant of the lynx
family.

THE JUNGLE CATS

Now we are going to come face to face with some of the most beautiful animals in the world. But don't let yourselves be bewitched by their eyes: they can be soft, tempestuous, compelling, of an almost indescribable luminous color somewhere between blue, green and yellow. These eyes belong to the tiger, the leopard, the panther, the jaguar and the cougar —to the lords of the jungle.

Magnificent in a yellow-gold coat striped with black, she makes her way with grace through the Asian jungle: it is the tiger. She moves lightly in spite of her nearly 550 pounds. She moves effortlessly over the ground, careful to step on stones, craftily placing her back paws in the tracks made by her front paws in order to confuse any possible follower. The tiger is above all a suspicious animal, so suspicious and crafty that no one, not even the cleverest and most fearless of hunters can take her unaware—not even when she sleeps. A nocturnal creature, the tiger begins hunting at sundown. And it is then that her luminescent and strangely hypnotic eyes scan the forest land so that she will be ready to glide like a snake or leap like an acrobat on any animal that comes within reach. There is but one

animal, the elephant, which can be careless about the tiger, and cross her path without fear. There is no other living creature able to escape the blood-thirsty killer tiger.

This lady of the night does not climb trees as the leopard does. But, like the jaguar, she is a capable swimmer. In fact, her daily diet, which consists of between 65 and 100 pounds of "meat" includes water creatures as well. The tiger eats standing up, always ready for an unpleasant surprise. In this she differs from the cheetah or the lion, which recline while eating, their muzzle buried deep in their——plate! Oops, I mean prey.

Tiger cubs, trained by their mother, soon learn to find their own food and avoid pitfalls and traps. This is why, as soon as they can fend for themselves, they go their own way in the jungle with an air of challenging the whole world.

According to a Malayan belief, the surest way to be caught by a tiger is to speak its name. For this reason in Malaysia and surrounding regions, the tiger is not called a tiger, but "the one with whiskers."

Across the page are two jaguars, so different looking at first glance. The male is in black and his mate in gold with black spots. Actually the male is not really jet black. In a certain light, spots are visible under his dark coat. Some natives fatten the jaguars and then eat them, believing that this will give them courage.

(above) The lynx, which is agile, patient and swift. In addition, he is supposedly the animal with the best eyesight. The oldest and most famous illustrations of academic societies, founded in 1603, chose the name Lincean (the lynxes) because its members were supposed to have the cleverness and perception of this animal.

Another distinctive and ferocious feline, this one found on the American continent is the puma. This too is an animal which strikes with its paws.

Well, boys and girls, why the puzzled look? I'm sure you've heard of the puma and the cougar too. The puma, the cougar, the American moutain lion, and the bear cat, even the silver cat, are all different names for the same magnificent animal. The puma is a roving bandit that is fleet and tireless, and completely formidable. He is also, ahem! something of a coward when he is chased or feels cornered by man or dogs. In captivity, that is, in zoos, he becomes quite tame, so much so that he permits visitors to approach. The puma or cougar seems to have a kind of love-hate feeling towards man. In fact, it is said that if he sees a man in danger, about to be attacked by a wild beast, he will come to the man's defense even at the cost of his own life.

Hey, watch out! Those two animals coming towards us are jaguars—a black panther and his beautiful spotted lady.

The jaguar is the real lord of the Amazonian jungle. He is a spectacular swimmer and prefers the jungle river banks where he finds most of his prey. He likes to stretch out on a branch overhanging the water, waiting for some large fish to swim by. He literally fishes for his meal with his paw. He is quite a gourmet, a ruthless hunter of capibara—large semi-aquatic rodent which live in the rivers of South America. The incisors of these rodents are often used as ornaments by the native people. The jaguar will hunt tapirs, ant-eaters and alligators if he cannot find anything he prefers. His victims are often domestic animals, which he catches at night by boldly jumping into cattle enclosures under the very eye of the watchman guarding the herds. The female jaguar usually gives birth to one to three cubs and looks after them lovingly for about two years.

Let us end this parade of these beautiful animals with the leopard—so splendid, magnificent, fierce, agile, elegant and fearless. The leopard, with the patience of Job, is able to lie in wait for hours and hours and hours. Balanced on a tree branch, once he has caught the scent of a possible victim, he will pounce on it like a hawk on his unwary prey.

The only rash motion—if we can call it that—which the wily leopard makes is to sharpen his talons on the trunks of trees, making it possible for the hunter to track him.

But now we should push on. There is someone making a lot of noise down there

At the left is a baby macaca, the most aggressive of all the monkeys. The famous monkeys who live on the Rock of Gibraltar belong to this family. They number about 30 and are the only monkeys found wild in Europe.

in the jungle. It isn't really a bellow—no, it is more like trumpeting. So we'll say goodby to the lovely, hypnotic, jade eyes of the jungle cats and be on our way.

THE BIGGEST OF THE LAND ANIMALS

That was a close shave! We just missed being bumped into by an elephant, and I personally almost lost my feathers, my spare ones included! Did you see what a race of giants they are, these elephants? One just doesn't joke with that kind of heavyweight. To think that at birth, poor mites, they only weigh around 200 pounds. But don't worry after a few years, our little ones will have no trouble at all carrying their six tons or so through the jungle as though it were nothing at all. And they won't break an arm or leg doing it, either.

An elephant's foot has five toes, and the animal walks, if you can call it that, on the tops of these, or rather on the nails. The bones of his feet are protected by a

sort of spongy sole which rests on the ground. This sole is so elastic and springy that when the elephant rests all his six ton weight on it, it gives like sponge, expanding when the foot is lifted. It's like a shock absorber!

Another feature of the elephant that is interesting is his trunk—and this is very much of an all-purpose instrument. He can sense which way the wind is blowing by lifting it up in the air like a peri-

At birth, an elephant is pink in color and is about 3 feet in height. In a few short hours he is able to stand, and in a few days can walk—with mamma's help. The mother is both kind and brave, and at the first sign of danger, she grabs her baby by the trunk and carries him to safety.
The elephants shown here are African. See the large ears, so different in size from the ears of elephants found in India. As you can see, Dumbo comes from Africa!

scope. And he can pluck fruit, branches and leaves when it is time to eat. He can drink with it, and search in dry terrain for water lying beneath the ground. He can draw sand up into his trunk and spray it on his back as a kind of daily anti-insect treatment. It is good to know that the elephant is a vegetarian, so much so that he consumes 500 lbs of fruit, leaves and barks of all kinds a day. He is not likely to go after the likes of you and me, friends.

If you look at an elephant's ears, you will be able to tell whether he comes from India or Africa! An African elephant is distinguished by his enormous floppy ears.

The Asian elephant is quite another matter. His ears are much smaller—in fact he is smaller altogether than his African relative. He is good-natured and a hard worker. We said worker, and we meant it, for he is often called the 'tractor' of the jungle. He is able to pull up to five tons of lumber without much effort. He works all day long together with his mahout, the man who rides on his head, who guides him, and tells him what to do and when. He is a good fellow, our little Asian elephant.

Oops, I almost forgot the pygmy elephant. He is even smaller, naturally, and is usually ignored by most people. Per-

haps this is because he is rarely taller than 5 feet and lives in the equatorial jungles of Africa. He differs from other elephants in that he is hairy—nearly as hairy as a monkey.

We might have known it. The elephants had hardly passed out of sight before the wart hog appeared in their tracks, hoping to pick up a meal without any effort. What can you do? The elephants allow him to do it, and go on to other things.

From the height of their wisdom they know that in life it is good to be lenient with those less fortunate. Finding his meals ready-made is small consolation for the wart hog, who, as one can guess from his name, is hardly a raving beauty. His generic name is Greek by derivation, and he does in fact have warts on his snout. What's more, when he senses danger he flees as fast as he can, his tail in the air like a flag. A hunter who is following almost has to stop and laugh, it looks so ridiculous.

In the jungles of South America, we come next to the giant armadillo of Bra-

zil. He really is a giant, measuring 5 feet in length and weighing in at around 140 pounds. There also is his cousin the 'pampas' armadillo, or "three-banded armadillo; as well as the nine-banded Mexican armadillo, or the 'cautious one,' because he digs many different lairs to confuse his enemies. All three of these armored boxes have one thing in common: a hard, banded hide which snaps closed. This well-sealed armor is this animal's best protection. In this way he can escape any foe except the natives, who have discovered a way of roasting the armadillo, armor and all.

We must also meet the giant anteater, surely one of the strangest mammals there is on earth. He belongs to the same group as the armadillo, but instead of armor, he is covered by thick fur. The giant anteater has a long, almost cylindrical snout,

The elephants across the page live in India. They need more than 300 quarts of water a day: 100 to quench their thirst; and 200 to pour over themselves.
(top, left) The wart hog has four large curved tusks and is remotely similar to the wild boar. (bottom, left) The large-eared armadillo—his name is the diminutive of the Spanish word 'armado' meaning armed.
(upper, right) On this page, a kind of squirrel, who is a born explorer and spends his time nosing around in the woods for nuts, acorns and pine cones.
(below) The tapir, who lives along the Amazon. He is a distant cousin of the horse and the rhinocerous.

with a very small mouth. His tongue is sticky and he flashes it out to catch ants, termites and other insects. Once he touches them with his tongue, they cannot escape. He can extend his tongue about 21 inches. The anteater's front paws have strong 'fingers' and extremely powerful claws that serve as an excellent defense against his sworn enemies, the jaguar and the puma. He often defeats these felines in battle—an anteater's hug can mean death. The young travel for a long time on their mother's back, and if they are attacked, she defends them with great courage. Even the lesser anteater, or tamandua, has dangerous claws and is a fierce fighter.

The flying squirrel parachutes from branch to branch in jumps as long as 100 feet.
(left) A roe buck, a small, nimble and graceful deer.
(right) The adorable koala bear, staring at us with a eucalyptus leaf in his mouth. He only eats the eucalyptus, and even more specifically, the particular oil contained in its leaves.

WHERE IT IS A LITTLE COOLER

The vegetation found in the forests of the temperate zones is much less luxurious than in the tropical jungles we have just left. But the oaks, chestnuts, poplars and beech trees that we find in them are of far greater use to us and, of course, are far more accessible. The animals that live in these forests are: deer of many varieties, boar, squirrels, dormice, martens, wildcats, and lynx. Here in the temperate regions it is wise to keep a scarf handy, because it can be very cold. Oof, I put a rattlesnake around my neck instead of a scarf! He lives in these forests too. What a mistake, though!

The animals we are visiting now have their own methods of keeping warm. Many of them make their homes underground. Others find shelter in hollow tree trunks. The fox, badger and groundhog, all burrow under the ground, while bears, for example, prefer a tree or even a cave. Otters dig into the river bank. The beaver,

for ever busy building dams, lives in a floating shelter, with an underground den for emergencies with several entrances under the water. We'll leave him there to his own devices and take a trip to another kind of forest.

IN THE SPICY PINE FOREST

A wide and impressive band of pine stretches from the southern forests to the northern tundra and covers the entire landmass of the northern hemisphere. This kind of forest land is also known under the name given to it by the Russians: the "taiga." The mammals found in these forests are: deer, elk, rodents, wolves, bears, and lynx.

As long as we are here, let's stop and visit a bit with the lynx. She lives in the coniferous forests of America, Asia, and parts of Europe. There are many kinds of lynx, but they all resemble one another. The color of their fur ranges from sand gray to a reddish brown spotted with black. In Europe, the lynx is also known as the deer wolf, and is slowly dying out. In certain regions of central and southern Spain it is still possible to catch a glimpse

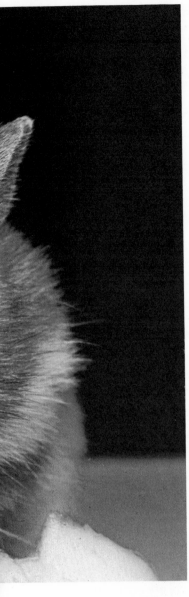

(center) The dormouse has but one worry and that is to keep his teeth in good shape. For this reason he eats continuously.

(above) The American Moose is often as tall as 6½ feet and can weigh half a ton. He lives in North America and Greenland. But in this picture he is not as impressive as he would be if full grown, for this is only a calf.

(opposite, left) The 'mouflon' is a species of wild sheep, the only one of its kind still found in Europe. In fact, these are only to be seen in Sardinia and Corsica.

of the leopard lynx, whose coat is yellow-brown with black spots. The lynx is an agile climber and daring leaper, with a great weakness for a diet of birds. In fact, he could eat them for breakfast, lunch and dinner. In Scandinavia and Siberia there is the Siberian lynx, and he is a real glutton, to say the least; for he kills more prey than he can eat. Besides that unpleasant trait, he has unusually wide paws, which serve him as 'snowshoes'.

The large Canadian lynx also had big wide paws, and boasts a beautiful, soft and silky coat. Because of it, he runs the continual risk of becoming some lady's

fur coat! The red American lynx, or bobcat, has a thick coat also. He hunts rats, which is useful and since his coat is not considered of much value, he is tolerated by man.

Here they are, boys and girls—the nicest citizens of the pine forests. They are the chipmunks, the hamsters, the squirrels and the dormice—also known as golden mice or walnut mice because of the color of their coat and their favorite food. The chipmunk is a charmer, with his soft, multi-colored coat. He is a member of the rodent family, with a small red and white face with two black stripes across it; his chest and belly are snow white, his tail is black and white, and his back is brown and black. He is unmistakable—and a chatterer. Shhh! Don't wake the dormouse! This rodent, small, grey-brown and white, stores away enormous amounts of acorns and other nuts in the autumn, and then goes to sleep for six months. When he wakes up, there is his food waiting for him.

Black bears are not shy. They do not hesitate to walk up to a car full of tourists and beg for a handout, like these in Yellowstone National Park. In spite of their weight they are agile enough, and when sensing danger, they climb a tree. They do this in the fashion of a boy shimmying up for a coconut—gripping the trunk with their forelegs and pushing themselves up by their hind legs. Once in the safety of the tree they snooze.
(opposite) Is the grizzly, who clearly prefers a more solid ground to lie on.

THE BEARS—FRIENDLY, BUT WATCH OUT!

Let's go, fast, before that bear swats us with his paw. Unless, of course, one of you happens to have a jar of honey handy? You have? Great, then we can arrange a meeting with the bears of the pine forest. Let us begin with the grizzly, who is seldom found except in Canada, the Alaskan wilds and national parks where he is protected. He is a brownish yellow color, able to walk for miles, and prefers to live close to a river so that he can swim, or fish for trout for dinner. Except for trout, the grizzly is actually a vegetarian, and lives off fruit, berries

and honey—and he includes bees as a side dish. Once greatly feared, this bear is a favorite today with the tourists in our national parks, and he will go right up to a car window to be fed.

Another favorite of the American continent is the black bear. Even though he is a good climber, runner and swimmer, he doesn't give the appearance of being much of an athlete, for he is very un-steady on his pins. In fact he isn't a sports-man at all, but just greedy. His favorite food is corn, and he will trespass onto whatever land he can find to steal a few ears off the stalk. He likes fish as well, and when it is time for the salmon to swim upstream to spawn, you'll find the black bear beside the rivers waiting for them. He adores his appetizers too, and if he runs out of shellfish, or shrimp, he'll

Species	Length In inches	Height in inches	Weight in lbs.	Litters per year	Number of Offspring per Litter	Gestation Period in days	Life Span
European Elk	112	112	2178	1	1-2	250	25
Antelope	103	103	2178	1	1-2	215-275	20
Ass	107	63	891	1	1	375	45
Blue Whale	1316	—	259,600	1	1	330	30
Barbary Ape	30	28	29	1	1	210	27
American Buffalo	119	72	3267	1	1	275	30
Oxen	119	56	3267	1	1-2	280	25
Buffalo	115	75	2178	1	1	340	16
Camel	135	72	1524	1	1	350-400	40
Chamois	58	31	85	1	1-2	165	20
Dog (Great Dane)	56	40	217	2	2-16	65	20
Kangaroo	59	72	217	1	1	40	13
Sperm Whale	872	—	174,240	1	1	480	25
Goat	65	31	173	1-3	2-3	150	10
Roe Buck	56	32	99	1	1-2	280	15
Beaver	40	—	66	1	2-6	128	20
Horse	131	72	2831	1	1-2	335	60
Boar	68	40	653	1	3-15	112	30
Domestic Rabbit	40	—	26	6-7	10-15	30	10
Wild Rabbit	18	—	3	3-4	4-10	30	13
Brown Fallow Deer	59	35	154	1	1	240	25
Red Fallow Deer	87	52	761	1	1-2	235	30
Weasel	9	—	.5	1-2	3-8	60	8
African Elephant	319	146	15,246	1	1	640	70
Seal	80	—	554	1	1-2	276	30
Giant Seal	278	—	6534	1	1	330	20
Ferret	15	—	2	2	5-10	60	13
Domestic Cat	22	12	8	2	3-6	60	20
Wild Cat	28	—	15	1	3-6	60	10
Gibbon	—	40	26	1	1	210	23
Giraffe	188	138	2178	1	1	440	28
Hyena	59	56	162	1	2-4	93	25
Hippopotamus	138	63	6534	1-2	1	240	41
Lama	96	108	290	1	1	330	20

The polar bear is different from other bears because he lives in the far north where it is always winter, and he does not hibernate.

Species	Length In inches	Height in inches	Weight in lbs.	Litters per year	Number of Offspring per Litter	Gestation Period in days	Life Span
Mamatee	119	—	1089	1	1-2	270	8
Lemur	19	—	—	1	1-2	60	20
Lion	108	40	506	1	2-4	106	40
Hare	28	—	11	2-4	2-5	42	10
Lynx	48	—	25	1	2-4	70	10
Otter	36	—	46	1-2	2-5	63	15
Wolf	44	32	132	1	3-9	63	16
Pig	100	47	1306	2-3	6-20	115	15
Groundhog	24	—	11	1	2-6	40	18
Moufflon	52	28	107	1	1-2	150	—
Opossum	22	—	11	2	9-12	13	8
Orangutan	—	53	173	1	1	260	50
Polar Bear	104	108	1306	1	1-2	250	34
Brown Bear	80	100	871	1 sì - 1 no	1-2	210-250	30
Panther	48	28	140	1	2-5	93	21
Sheep	60	32	325	1	1-2	150	14
Bat	18	68	2	1	1	60	15
Sea Pig (Walrus?)	80	—	110	1	1	360	15
Porcupine	22	—	33	—	2-3	112	20
Gray Rat	10	—	1	2-7	5-14	22	5
Reindeer	92	56	435	1	1	246	15
Hedgehog	12	—	2	1-2	3-7	60	5
Rhinoceros	200	72	4360	1 sì - 1 no	1	560	40
Chimpanzee	—	56	162	1	1	270	50
Squirrel	9	—	1	2	3-6	32-40	15
Ibex	60	37	237	1	1-2	150	30
Mole	6	—	.02	1-2	3-7	40	3
Tapir	80	40	653	1 sì - 1 no	1	390	30
Badger	31	—	25	1	3-5	180	15
Tiger	80	40	475	1 sì - 1 no	1	106	25
Rat	4	—	.01	4-6	4-8	21	4
Spider Mouse	3	—	.01	1	5-10	20	2
Fox	32	15	22	1	3-8	54	14
Zebra	76	60	693	1	1	375	30

settle for a frog or two, some ants, or even termites. All of course balanced by ripe fruit and vegetables. But what the black bear is really crazy for is pork chops. Imagine! And since no one is likely to deliver them to him ready cooked, he occasionally helps himself to an entire pig, from the nearest farm.

Newborn bears are about the size of small rabbits. After three or four months, they will take their first steps, but are cared for by their mother for a whole year. After that, or so it is said, it is their turn to look after baby sister and brother.

Well, boys and girls, our journey through the jungles and woods is over. The bear is napping, so I think we'll leave him to it and go on.

33

BEASTS OF THE OPEN COUNTRY

Here I am again. Your old friend Donald Duck and I have to admit that I feel more like a cat than ever! I've been planning a marvelous adventure for you. We'll let the wind blow us through prairies and deserts, over plains and tundra, and we will meet all the animals along the way, who live in these wide open spaces.

LET'S LOOK AROUND

The wide open spaces, whether plains, deserts, or steppes, have one thing in common: the absence, or partial absence, of trees, depending on the amount of moisture in the air and in the earth. We are going to see all of them, from the relatively damp areas—the plains of Africa, the Brazilian campos, to the north American prairies, the steppes of Central Asia, and the arid deserts and semi-deserts.

Let us take a look at the similarities between the animals living in these places, and see how they have adapted to life there.

Sorry, friends. I get carried away in my fondness for botany and climate. True, these subjects are not only important in themselves, but are also bound closely with the lives of men and animals. But we must stick to our journey.

And so I'll make it simple and say that the steppes and the plains have a great deal of grass and bushes. Above all, there is a vast amount of space, where animals move in herds and flocks and where one can see for miles and miles.

The lion lives on the plains and the steppes, and so do the zebras and the antelopes. Of course. I say, of course, because the zebras and the antelopes feed off the bushes and the grass; but the lions feed on the zebras and antelopes.

CATS OF THE OPEN GRASSLANDS

Now boys and girls, we are going to join the animals of the open lands. Be careful, though, to move against the wind, so that the lion will not scent us. We are hoping to see him and have him wander away without knowing we're there. It would be too bad if all our travels ended now after all my trouble!

The lion. . . . How does he look? Since most of us have some idea of what the lion is like, let us start off with him. From the tip of his nose to the tuft at the end of his tail, he's about 10 feet long, and about 3 feet high, from shoulder to ground. He weighs between 325—500 pounds. Only the male has a mane, full around his head and falling down around his shoulders. It is about one and a half feet long. The lioness is a slender mane-less copy of her mate. Both have a tail that ends in a fur tuft, under which is a sort of claw. When irritated by flies, or angry, the lion whips his tail against his flanks. Our cats at home do the same thing, but because they are perhaps more clever, they merely give their tail a flick. Like our cats too, the lion will nibble on grass when his insides are out of order. But he is carnivorous and his favorite food is meat, raw, and preferably fresh—some beast he has killed that day. During most of the daylight hours, the lion lies in the shade of some acacia tree or rolls on the grass with his fellows. It is only when night falls that the swift and silent lion hunts. He is always careful to move up wind and so is able to surprise the zebra, gazelle, buffalo and other animals who are his victims. Unlike the tiger, leopard and similar cats the lion kills only for food and never for the sport of killing itself. It is always the male who eats first. When he has had his fill, the lioness and cubs have their turn.

What's left is put aside in a special place, for next day. Once he has eaten, and is satisfied, the lion is relatively harmless. He wouldn't even take the trouble to

swat at a lamb, should it walk under his nose. In the home of the lion, it is the lioness who rules. She is a terror and can make a lot of trouble, especially when her cubs are around. Her mate, poor fellow, must stay clear of his children until they are several weeks old. Then with permission and under the stern and protective eye of the lioness, he is allowed to play a little with his cubs. Always, of course, if

Lions show their social nature by living in families instead of herds as other animals do. The families are usually made up of from six to twenty animals, and the father lion is king. The lionesses are good to all the young and often nurse cubs belonging to other mothers. The cubs stay with their mothers for about two years, that is, until they have learned the art of hunting and killing their prey without risking a kick in the face from a zebra. The zebra's only defenses are his hooves, speed, good sense of smell and good eyesight.

Gliding silently over the plains, the leopard, whom we see above, prefers to sneak up unseen. When he is just a few feet away, he pounces on his prey and has fresh meat for the day. One creature the leopard can't count on for his meal is the maned porcupine. When it senses danger, this spiky mammal curls itself into a ball, with all its quills pointed, and waits for better times. The maned porcupine lives in Sicily, in the Balkans, and in North and East Africa and weighs up to 40 lbs.
(At the right) Cheetahs gathered together for a family reunion: they're beginning to feel hunger pains. In democratic fashion, they'll all share in plans for a hunt. They meet around a "common tree," marked by their claw scratches.
(far right) A fennec, or desert fox. Although he is in a dreamy, half-awake state, his ears are fully alert to catch the slightest danger signal.

there is no "tiger horse" in sight.

"Tiger horse", you ask? Don't be puzzled. This is just an old name for the zebra. This animal, like his enemy, the lion, likes the wide open spaces where he can canter and kick and gambol with other zebras. You may think that all zebras look alike. This is not the case at all, for the color of their stripes varies considerably —from a very light pink shade to brown, off-white, dark yellow and black stripes of differing widths. Zebras are generally gregarious, assembling in herds of 10 to

12 or else mingling in herds of other animals such as wildebeests or even ostriches.

The main concern of the zebra is water. If he could manage to do without the daily walk to the waterhole at dawn, he might live to the age of 28 years. But every day he goes after water, and every other day the lions sits there and waits. Every second day he—the lion —digests his food.

Hey, watch out! Here come the cheetahs, racing by at full speed. Since this cat sprints at 65 mph without any effort at all, you'll feel quite a draft. All

of you probably know the cheetah's funny face. But did you know that because he is so active a sportsman he often loses his claws. They are rubbed so much against the ground that the claw muscles gradually degenerate—that is, deteriorate. This never happens to any of the other cats. The poor cheetah has no claws to use in attacking his prey or in defending himself. But he isn't much of an eater, in fact quite the opposite, since he can go for days between one meal and the next. This may be why the cheetah weighs a mere 125 pounds.

Cheetahs love their family dearly, and in spite of their race into the distance, they always remember to come home. During their "cubhood" cheetahs are not very sure of themselves, and stay close to their mother for about two years. You can be sure there is no rebellion in the family. The cheetah, even as a cub, is gentle and affectionate. He is this way towards man also. It is a pity than man appreciates this animal's fur more than his disposition and so hunts him down.

THE THIRSTY DESERT

How strange, it seems to me that we are in the desert. I bet we arrived here chasing after a cheetah. I didn't plan to be here just yet, but since we are, I'll introduce you to the fennec. He looks sleepy, doesn't he? And I doubt that he knows we're here. The fennec sleeps all day long. What is he? Why, the desert fox, of course. His ears are enormous in proportion to the rest of him, and they allow him to hear the slightest noise. At the sound of anything threatening he digs furiously into the ground to hide.

His Majesty, the lion, after a good meal.
His wide-awake companions are the hyena (above)
and the jackal (below). They live on the lion's
leftovers.

His legs kick so rapidly that an on-looker would find it hard to distinguish his movements. As I told you, he sleeps all day. When he wakes up at night, he has a drink and then goes on the hunt, for lizards, rodents and other substantial food. If he can't find what he wants, he'll settle for a lighter snack, such as birds eggs, or dates. Seriously, let us take a look at this animal, whose tail, body and head together don't even measure more than 1½ feet. His ears are as wide and as long as the entire head. It is really thanks to his smallness, though, that the fennec can survive in such an unfriendly habitat. The desert, where he lives, contains snakes and insects all able to live in the hottest of climates with very little water. Desert mammals don't require much water. Like rodents, they do not sweat a great deal, and their bodies have clever mechanisms allowing them to store the water they drink. Many antelopes, orycteropi and armadillos are able to survive for a long time without drinking a drop. They satisfy their thirst with the liquid they find in plants and in the animals they eat.

The camel and the dromedary, both 41

The Amercan badger, or carcajou, digs his den with his short legs.

proverbially able to go for long periods without water, actually are less equipped to resist thirst than we think, and are only able to last for twenty days or so without water.

Elephants are only able to go without water for about three or four days.

AGAINST THE DESERT HEAT AND COLD

Rapid temperature changes are very characteristic of the open plains. This is the case not only from season to season, but often from day to night as well. In Africa a forty degree variation in temperature is very possible, while freezing temperatures are not uncommon even in the Sahara Desert. In Tibet, summer temperature can rise to 40° at noon, and drop to 37° below in winter. In these kinds of conditions life on the land's surface for cold-blooded animals becomes a difficult business. Even warm-blooded animals must find a means of protecting themselves against sudden temperature changes.

One effective method of survival under such hardship is to live underground, in tunnels or holes dug into earth or sand. At about 1½ feet below the surface, it is noticeably cooler in summer and

warmer in winter. And so the desert animals, rodents chiefly, live underground—especially in day time. Typical of these below-ground rodents is the prairie-dog, a kind of marmot found in North America, and the Alpine pika or whistling hare of the Mongolian steppes. Pikas are far-sighted. They also plan ahead, digging holes and using them and cracks to store the hay and herbs which are their favorite food. Many mammals, because they live in this sort of environment, have greatly developed endurance and speed. Because these animals must cover long distances to reach water and must be ready for quick escape from their enemies, they have developed as much as is possible their ability to run and jump.

I can't tell you which sort of flight I'd use if I were being chased by a cheetah, or even by the slower lion. After all, we ducks are somewhat handicapped. I only know that I'd do my utmost to save myself, and keep my feathers intact.

Let's return to the matter of sports. Some animals prefer to leap rather than

42

run, and can go faster this way. The most notable of this type of animal is the Australian kangaroo (or most of them) and other jumping marsupials. Many rodents in different parts of the world have a similar body structure, that is, their rear legs and tail (which they use to lean on and to keep their balance) are highly developed. With the exceptions of South America and Europe, there are jumping mice all over the world: in Africa, Asia, Australia and North America.

FRIENDLY ALLIES

On the open plains you can see for long distances, and nearly all the inhabitants have excellent eyesight and very acute hearing. It is above all, the sense of sight that is important when it

A curious battle between the rattlesnake and kangaroo mouse who, as soon as he sees the enemy jumps straight up in the air. Before attacking the snake, the mouse calmly smooths his whiskers; then, when the rattlesnake flicks his black tongue, the small mouse throws sand on him with his four paws.

comes to community living. By this I mean the tendency to collect in groups of large numbers. This is particularly evident among the animals who live on the open plains in herds: the antelopes, the buffalos, zebras and guanacos. Not only that: this herd may be made up of more than one species. The hemionos of Central Asia are nearly always found in the company of wild sheep, for example. The Tibetan antelope and yak are usually together. Hyenas and jackals hunt in groups, sometimes even with the lion. The giraffe . . .

I think we'll stop a moment and talk at greater length about the giraffe. First of all, since we were on that subject before, I want to tell you that the giraffes too live in groups with other animals such as zebras, various kinds of antelopes, gazelles and ostriches.

A giraffe has a long neck—a very long neck. Altogether they are about 16-18 feet tall. Because of their height and their exceptionally good eyesight, they serve as lookout for the rest because they can spot an enemy a long way off. In spite of their natural shyness and peace-loving disposition, they know how to defend themselves against the big cats who every now and then attempt to attack them. In fact, their hooves are lethal and a lion who has tangled with them once will seldom try it again. Although peaceful, giraffes live in groups with a social structure all their own. The leader of the group is the only one allowed to cut in front of another when they are traveling along; he is highly respected by his fellow giraffes, who hardly dare sniff the air in his presence. Speaking of the giraffe, I must tell you that he has a heart as big

44

The peccary (below) have a highly developed social sense. They live in groups and communicate among themselves to form a tight mass in case of danger.

as all outdoors, as they say. In actual fact, the heart of this animal weighs more than 23 pounds and is able to pump about 51 ½ quarts of blood per minute. You must understand, my friends, that this force is necessary, to pump the blood all the way up that long neck until it reaches the brain. Too rapid a rush of blood to the head, though, might cause an immediate congestion of the brain and therefore death. And so when the giraffe bends its neck down to drink, its circulation is regulated by special valves. As soon as it lowers its head below its body, the safety valves close and prevent the flow of blood to the brain. Arabs call the giraffe "zarafah", that is, "amiable creature who walks with a sure tread".

This description of a sure and graceful

The black and white African rhinoceros we see here are the only animals not afraid of fire. Instead of running off in fright or steering clear of camp fires lit to keep animals away, they become angry and attack.

Rhinos are dangerous because they are "sudden" and unpredictable. An unusual feature of the white rhino is a lower lip as hard as his tusk, to cut through the tough grasses he eats.

step certainly cannot be applied to the rhinocerus. Even the eyesight of this poor ugly animal isn't very good. To compensate for this, boys and girls, he has a thick skin! So thick is this skin, as a matter of fact, that the natives, when they manage to remove it from the animal, make shields from it that not even a lance or scimitar could penetrate. Perhaps we'd better talk about these dangerous animals right now and get it over with so that we can pass on to the rest undisturbed!

Both the black and the white African rhinos have two horns. The horns of the black measure 2 ⅓ feet and 1 ⅔ feet respectively; the horns of the white rhino measure 4 feet and 2 feet. The India rhino has only one horn, measuring 2 feet; the Sonda rhino has one 1 foot horn; the Sumatra two horns, one 2 feet long, the other ⅔ of a foot. All horns, whether big, medium, or small, are used by the animal to gore his enemy. Let's stay clear of this beast and move on. We have a good chance, because he can't see much beyond his nose—in fact his vision reaches about 100 feet. His hearing is excellent, in part because of the shape of his ears which resemble old fashioned ear trumpets. Ever seen one? To show off for his relatives, the tapir and the horse, the rhino trots about on his funny but agile hooves. The rhino's skin, in spite of its thickness, is very sensitive to insect bites. To rid himself of insects, the animal soaks himself in a pond or stream. When he is not able to reach water he keeps a layer of mud on his skin. When this mud dries, it forms

45

a protective covering. The most persistent of the insects are disposed of by the bufagas who'll eat almost anything. They perch on the rhino's back and have a feast.

Friend's, you'll be thinking that Donald has a weakness for rhinos, because I've gone on so long about them. The truth is I'm trying to be fair to all my new acquaintances. One last word; I bet you didn't know that once the Chinese believed if you put poison into a cup made of rhinocerus horn, the drink would boil up spontaneously. Just remember that!

African buffalo, are also
called black buffalo because
of their color. Wild and
untamable, this buffalo
fears only the lion, which
he sometimes succeeds in
striking and killing. In the
two photographs below:
antelope. There are so
many types of antelope and
gazelle and they run in
such large herds, that it is
difficult even for specialists
to distinguish each indi-
vidual type within the
numerous families.

FAKING DEAD—TO STAY ALIVE

There's only one way to behave if you're around the African buffalo, and that is to play dead. I mean if you shot at the animal and missed him. Really, it is the buffalo who plays dead to survive. This happens when the buffalo, alive after a hunter's near miss, realizes that there will be another shot coming. The animal drops to the ground. The hunters, of course, believe that he is really dead and approach to admire their prey—when all of a sudden. . . . You can take my word for it, if those hunters don't get away fast, its the end for them.

THE WONDERFUL STEPPES

I wish it were otherwise, but having to talk now about the steppes makes me feel completely helpless. So I have asked for reliable information from someone else. I've called on Ludwig von Drake. He was in good form and talked for twenty-four hours on end. Here I am, tired but happy, and ready to pass it all on to you.

The steppes—what a magic sound it has! And to think that all it is, is grass, green in the rainy season and yellow and arid in the dry season. This sort of terrain is known as prairie in North America, Pampas in Argentina, puszta in Hungary, and lande in France, and in southeastern Europe and Asia steppes.

The Eurasian steppes are vast, stretching from Hungary and southern Russia and extending across all of central Asia.

(top, left) Two surprised and alarmed prairie dogs. These rodents are tireless diggers and their tunnels are often as deep as 16 feet.
(left) The mará or Patagonian hare.
(opposite, above) These single humped camels, are ownerless and unbranded. They roam freely over the deserts of Arabia, North Africa, and the Middle East.

48

There is similar terrain, though on a smaller scale, in South Africa, Australia and Patagonia.

In the dry earth of this vast region there lives a strange rodent that is something like a hare, but which actually is a close relative of the guinea pig. It is called the mará or Patagonian hare. During the day this animal remains hidden in a deep, underground hole, but at night he's up and about. He comes up to graze with friends and relatives—and even in the smallest of spaces, they munch together on grass roots and tubers. The mara's hind legs are long, and so he is a high jumper. These athletic traits make him interesting game for hunters, unfortunately.

After 1900, when poachers in Yellowstone National Park killed sixteen of the remaining 20 head of bison, naturalists believed that the American bison was doomed to die out. Only a few decades earlier, thousands and thousands of bison had roamed free over the prairies. When the West was won, bison were killed by the thousand. But when it became known that only four had survived, many zoos sent their bison to join the survivors so that the species wouldn't die out. Today there are about 30,000 living bison. A typical South American animal is the llama, photographed below. Notice the long neck, small size, and absence of hump, even though this animal is related to the camel. The llama can carry loads of up to 100 lbs. at altitudes that no other animal would survive.

In the steppes, the abundance of animal life depends directly upon the vegetation. Every bit of it is used for food, from the roots to the tips of blades of grass. Since the bushes are sometimes thorny and tough, obviously good chewing ability is an asset. Rodents and ungulates (horses, antelopes and buffaloes—animals with hooves) have sharp front teeth. These enable them to cut leaves and branches. They also have strong molars with which to chew their food. The problem of water is solved by the use of fat plants, such as cactus—which provides both food and water at the same time. When, however, the last water hole dries up, the animals of the steppes must move away.

When the land is covered with snow there are other problems of survival: chief of them is the ability to resist the cold. The animals which suffer the least are the larger mammals with thick fur and a reserve of fat. The buffalo, the yak, and wild camel can even afford to play in the snow. But the other animals are forced to migrate. Antelopes and wild donkeys leave the Gobi desert not because of snow, but because the water freezes over. The trails made by bison across the North American plains during their regular migrations were once famous.

Let's talk a little about this fine big beast who is the North American buffalo. Come with me to Yellowstone National Park, where at last the bison is able to live in peace, protected and almost spoiled by those looking after their "august persons." What do the keepers do? Simple: when the temperature drops below zero and hits -4 (F), when the snow is piled high in drifts, the keepers deliver hay by the ton to every bison.

Now it seems as though the snow here has covered everything with a white blanket. I'll take immediate advantage of the situation and ask you to pay special attention to the following tracks. Yes, I said tracks.

FOOTPRINTS WE CAN FOLLOW

Bears are called plantigrades *because when they walk they place their weight on the soles of their feet. Thanks to this large "support" area, they are able to walk erect. The paws of plantigrades have five fingers with long, heavy non-retractable claws. The polar bear's fingers are joined at the base by a membrane which facilitates swimming. Canidae, or the dog family, use only the toes of their paws to walk on. These toes five to the forepaws and four to the hindpaws, have rather straight non-retractable claws. Insectivorous animals (those who feed on*

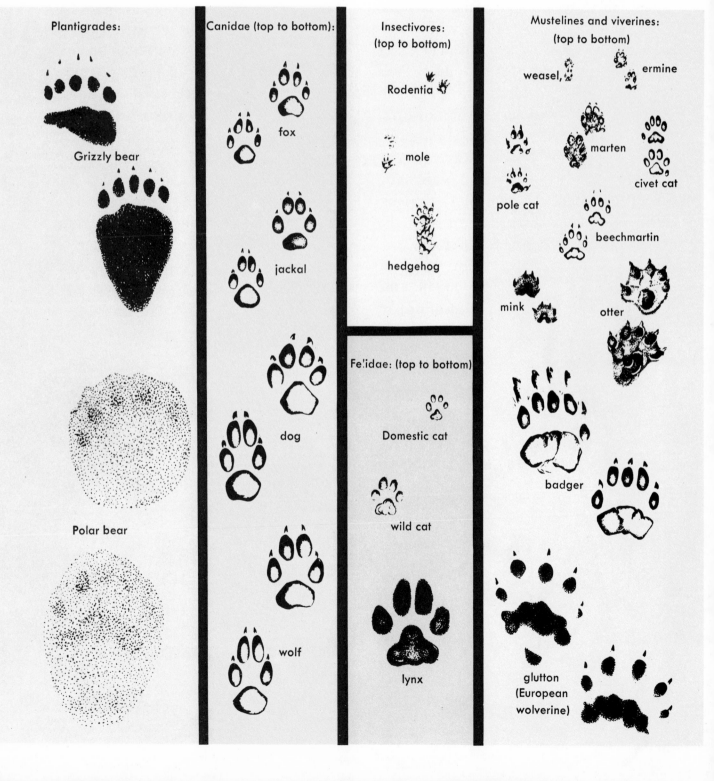

Plantigrades:

Grizzly bear

Polar bear

Canidae (top to bottom):

fox

jackal

dog

wolf

Insectivores: (top to bottom)

Rodentia

mole

hedgehog

Fe!idae: (top to bottom)

Domestic cat

wild cat

lynx

Mustelines and viverines: (top to bottom)

weasel, ermine

pole cat

marten

civet cat

beechmartin

mink

otter

badger

glutton (European wolverine)

insects) have short, five-fingered paws facing outward to make it easy to dig and remove earth. Felidae are various members of the cat family, and have large, almost, chubby five-fingered paws on the front legs and four-fingered paws on the hind legs. The nails are thin and retractable (can be drawn in).

The mustelines have small paws with four or five fingers and retractable nails. Hunters are easily able to distinguish the many different paw prints, not because they love science and have studied them, but because they love furs. Viverines are civets and similar to mustelines.

Ungulates are hooved animals. Rodents in general have very strong paws with sharp, curved nails.

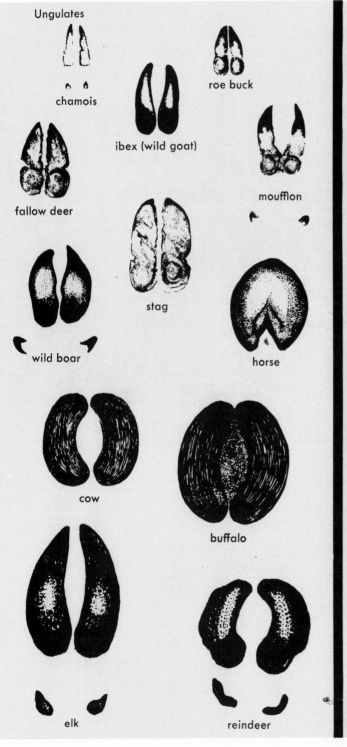

Ungulates

chamois — ibex (wild goat) — roe buck — moufflon — fallow deer — stag — wild boar — horse — cow — buffalo — elk — reindeer

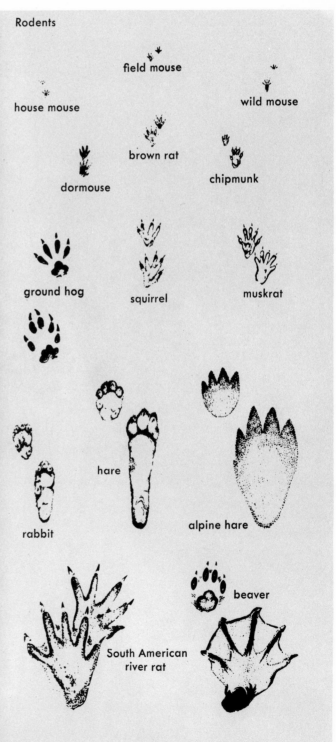

Rodents

house mouse — field mouse — wild mouse — dormouse — brown rat — chipmunk — ground hog — squirrel — muskrat — rabbit — hare — alpine hare — beaver — South American river rat

DRESSED TO MATCH THEIR SURROUNDINGS

Boys and girls, I've thought up a trip that would be the envy of the hardiest of travel agents. Are you with me? This is what I've planned: we'll explore regions where no one goes except in error. We'll tour the swamps. I'll show you the tundra. We'll take a look at the shores of rivers, lakes, and seas. I have something for everyone, whatever his tastes.

Let us begin by taking a careful look at the environment. Animal life in swamps and along shores is characterized chiefly by the abundance of water. There is always plenty of food, and it is so tasty that it attracts large numbers of animals. Naturally, many of these animals are aquatic and know how to swim. For many of the animals, there are in addition to the aquatic vegetation, inexhaustible reserves of insects. And what marvelous reserves they are. Just think, boys and girls, that in summer, strange as it may seem, the tundras of North America, Asia and America are literally blackened by gnats, mosquitoes, horseflies and sand flies. These are a real menace to the unlucky traveler who has come without an insect repellent!

For the animals, the water serves also as a refuge—both from the heat and from their enemies. And it is also a hunting preserve, which the animals leave to return to the land once their bellies are full. It is interesting to see how nature solves the problem in similar ways for different groups of animals. For example, the hippopotamus, the frog, and the crocodile all have eyes and nostrils that are similarly shaped. All three of these animals are able to remain under water for at least a half hour, if not more, but must come up for air and look around for food. To do this, they peer out from just below the surface of the water with their nostrils and eyes, apparently made to order for this purpose.

One of the most interesting animals of this type, and one of the best adapted, is the Australian platypus, the only mammal with a duck's bill. There are many animals who live around rivers, lakes and swamps: the beaver, nutria, otter and muskrat. This small fellow, the muskrat, was originally from North America. Prized for its fur, it was introduced in Europe—Czechoslovakia to be precise—around 1905. Today the muskrat has extended its territory and can be found from France to Kamchatka in Russia. People are of different opinions as to the value of this animal in the humid regions of Eurasia.

In Western Europe, for example, where the muskrat digs deep burrows along river banks and at the edges of dams, he is naturally considered a pest who causes damage. This is particularly the case when we remember that the muskrat is continually active, day and night. But there are regions where his fur is much sought after and where therefore he has value as a source of income.

But let me add, boys and girls, that among other animals of the coastal regions are seals and otters, although these mammals are usually found in the sea and seek dry land only to reproduce. I'll have more to tell you about seals and otters when we reach the polar regions.

Swamps and river banks are frequented also by the ungulates—those mammals with hooves—such as tapirs, many kinds of antelopes, reindeer, elk, caribou and Asian buffalo. Most of these are herbivorous animals (they do not eat meat) and contribute to maintaining their environment by keeping the vegetation at the right balance. Otherwise, if it all grew freely, many areas would dry up.

This makes the animals a sort of an ally to man. Another example is found with the hippopotamus!

THE WATER LORDS

No, my friends, really there is no need to look so surprised. Pay attention to what I say, and I'm sure you'll even become fond of the hippopotamus.

The strange-looking duckbill platypus lives in Australia and Tasmania and has a flat tail similar to the beaver's and very short legs. His body is shaped like a sausage and his 'hands' and 'feet' are enormous, with five fingers each and strong claws. His hind paws have 'palms' right up to the base of his nails, and on the front paws the membrane covers the nails (see photo at right). His head is most unusual with no ears. His hearing ducts and eyes are closed by wrinkles in the skin. His mouth is shaped like a duck's bill and is as flexible as rubber.

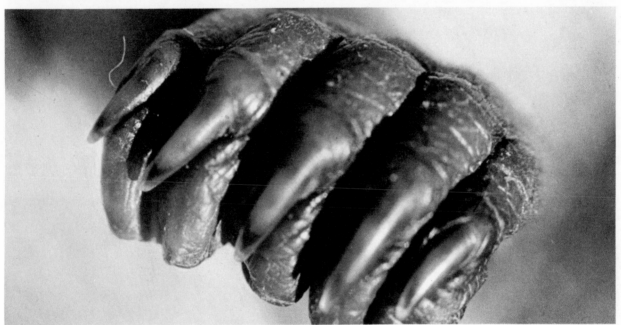

You may not know it, but there was a time when the hippopotamus lived undisturbed in the swamps of Africa—particularly in the Congo.

But little by little, as trees were cut down and vast areas put into cultivation, a sort of conflict of interests was created between man and the hippopotamus. For their part, during the night the animals staged real invasions into the fields in search of juicy roots and forage. And for man the password was: destroy the hippopotamus—and from the word to the deed the step was short.

For a time things seemed to go as ordered, but as is usually the case when man tampers with the balance of nature, another problem arose that was much more serious. This problem was known by the poetic name of "water-lily". This ordinary floating plant happened to be one of the hippopotamus' favorite tidbits, and unconsumed, it began to invade the rivers of central Africa. The waterlily choked the rivers to such a degree that navigation became dangerous, if not downright impossible. Since obviously navigation is necessary, attempts are now

57

The capybara is the largest living rodent, weighing up to 200 lbs. The one shown above is a cub. The Indian buffalo (below) is an excellent beast of burden in marshy regions.

being made to bring the hippopotamus back to those regions from which he was chased.

This water lily is not only a problem in terms of navigation. It is actually dangerous to man because it makes possible the reproduction of certain water snails that are hosts to a worm parasitic to man.

DRUMBEAT OF THE BUSY BEAVER

Many mammals that live in swamps have a flat tail. This tail looks very strange, but it is very useful to its owner in swimming and also helps him when he must make an escape. Let's take the beaver, for example.

It's no secret that the otter (above) would rather live in water than on land. He can stay underwater for great lengths of time and when he surfaces, he barely sticks his nose out. He isn't bothered by cold and he is a very playful clown. At right, a close-up of the hippopatamus, his eyes sticking up out of the water like a periscope. Perhaps there is an intruder lurking in the area, and the hippo is watching him.

I knew one once—I met him in Montana —who owned a 2,000 foot dam (this size dam must have beaten the record!). Well, this beaver's tail was long, flat and scaly. He told me, my friend in Montana, that it serves as a helm when he swims, a prop when he sits, and as a means of defense. I 60 don't mean that the beaver uses his tail

The beaver has fascinated man since prehistoric times and has influenced our life in many ways. Building his dams, the beaver has created ponds, which, filling up with debris, after many thousands of years form immense pastures and fertile plains. The two photographs (opposite and right) show the shape of the beaver's paw and tail. There is the velvet-antlered caribou (top, opposite), a close relative of the reindeer, though not the same size.

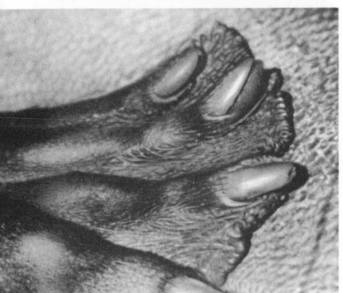

when he's attacked to slap his enemy around. He does use it to slap the water like a drum major. The sound serves as an order for his companions, all busy at work building houses, to dive beneath the surface. In fact, the beavers obey the drumming. They drop their tools (if they have them) and dive to safety.

However, in spite of this organized warning system, the beaver, once very common, almost disappeared from the face of the earth. This was due to man's handiwork, for he had discovered just how soft and valuable the beaver's fur could be. Matters have improved somewhat. Here in North America, the beaver has a more peaceful life than in the past, because we have learned at last that indiscriminate slaughter of animals can only hurt us in the long run. And in Norway, France and in the Rhone valley of Germany, the beaver lives proudly and happily protected by laws.

A SMALL HOME OF BRANCHES

When he has picked the spot he likes along the river banks, the beaver faces the problem of building his "home sweet home" The intelligent, resourceful and industrious beaver wants his house to be useful, safe, and elegant. When it's time for work to begin, the beavers vanish into the woods. There they collect and prepare the necessary raw materials. Each beaver, with the help of his four, strong, sharp, front teeth, cuts down trees, severs the branches and strips the bark. Not only do they strip the bark, they eat it as well, since it is their staple diet. Then using all his strength in a sort of assembly line operation, each beaver carries a tree trunk or branch to the building site where the other beavers wait, to carry on with the construction itself. With the skill and experience of an engineer, and the imagination, of an architect, these beavers make such that each part of the house suits the purpose it is meant to serve. The living-room is always above water level, while the entrance—a tunnel about 15 to 20 feet long—begins underwater. There is also a service entrance—a larger tunnel than the first—through which wood is dragged and stored away for food. Please note that although part of the house is underwater, it is perfectly dry, because Father beaver has put down a sort of mat at the front entrance. Here the beavers dry their feet and shake their fur out—down to the last drop of water. The water drips from this mat to the ground beneath it. The living room stays dry and beavers don't get rheumatism. When the house is finished the beavers check the dams—which were built beforehand—to make sure they are still in good condition and won't flood.

A WELL-PROTECTED NEST

The platypus too is a clever builder. He is by nature a complicated fellow, and so his den couldn't be anything else but very complicated indeed. Some dens are living quarters for the whole family. Others are reserved for the females to lay their eggs and raise their offspring; this section is built near the water, with many entrances hidden near the roots of nearby trees. The other sections are really long tunnels, which surface just above water level. The house is equipped with two entrances that lead to the "nursery". Mother platypus won't leave it though, until she's finished nursing her little ones.

HUNTED BUT HAPPY

Isn't the Big Bad Wolf going to hibernate this winter? Apparently not. Instead he's gone a little crazy and looks as though he'd rather hunt a Lonely Duck than the Three Little Pigs, or even three little raccoons. Ah well, let's take a look at the raccoons, who may have eaten your corn this summer if you were growing any.

This native of areas that lie around the swamps and creeks is very intelligent and even friendly. That funny little face staring at us with its odd mask is an excellent camouflage for defense. It is nature's way of hiding the animal's most vulnerable spot, his eyes, from the enemy. The raccoon, my friends, is very vulnerable indeed, because his fur is so beautiful to look at, and warm too. This means that he spends a good part of his life running and hiding from hunters, traps, and dogs. All this taken into account, he is pretty happy-go-lucky; his thoughts center around getting all the food he can into his paws. Fortunately, he has remarkably skillful paws, which are capable of carrying along his somewhat chubby body at a swift pace if necessary.

Our raccoon loves the air of the swamp. He eats frogs, shrimps and other shellfish, and varies this diet with corn—ah, how he loves sweet corn—eggs, fruit, meat, and nuts. He is a glutton, and always famished, but he is nevertheless very clean about his food. He always washes the morsels before popping them into his mouth—this is of course if he is near a stream! So he achieves a double purpose: he gets rid of the mud which covers frogs and crayfish, and he moistens the tidbits which he might otherwise have trouble swallowing for lack of saliva.

AMONG THE MOSS AND LICHEN

Right now, why don't we go for a breath of air in the tundra? What's that? You don't feel like it? Well, my friends, if you think that after I've read up on all

A trio of funny-faced raccoons. (left). They are usually wild and aggressive animals. When frightened, the raccoon emits very strange sounds indeed, something like a long whistle, but so high-pitched it's almost inaudible to the human ear. The raccoon, if intelligently trained, makes a good house pet. Graceful, elegant, and eager, the ermine has a reddish-brown coat during the summer (right) and a white one, except for the dark tip of its tail, in winter (above). The ermine's fur is characteristically soft and shiny. He belongs to the mustelidae family, many of whom, experts believe, hold funerals for their dead, dragging them away with much ceremony. Skunks, minks, and marten are among the mustelidae. All are small and carnivorous, with valuable fur.

A beautiful specimen of the badger (left) caught in a very characteristic act. As he drinks, the badger doubtless has his mind on his daily clean-up. He lives in one of the cleanest, neatest dens you could ever wish to visit. An elk, cropping grass (above). Graceful Canadian deer at the edge of the woods (below). An otter (bottom, right) in the snow, with a clever, intelligent little face. Note his paws with their webbed membrane.

the moss and lichen that grow in the tundra I'm going to give it a miss, you're just wrong.

So—the tundra is land covered by dwarf plants, like moss and lichen. Sometimes all of it is covered by snow and ice. The tundra regions are: the Yenisei basin (the Yenisei is a Siberian river flowing into the Arctic Sea); the coastal areas and the islands which face the Bering sea; Greenland; the region around the Hudson Bay, and the islands surround that the Arctic poles.

Why is it that moss and lichen alone grow in these parts? That's an easy one to answer. It is because the soil just beneath the earth's surface is nearly always frozen and no other vegetation can grow because it cannot put down deep roots. The tundra covers the Arctic regions of the North hemisphere where living conditions are severe in winter. So clearly only warm-blooded animals like birds and mammals are able to live there all year round. Warm-blooded animals have a constant body temperature and are independent of their habitat. Small mammals such as the lemmings, fox, and arctic hare,

are protected against the cold by a sort of double fur; the layer closest to the skin is very thick and wooly. The coat of the musk ox is made up of long fur which gives him a protective covering right down to his paws. He also has a thick layer of fat which keeps in his body heat. In similar fashion, the Arctic hare becomes very fat when winter comes. In contrast, his brother, the European hare, who is not exposed to such great cold, remains lean throughout the year.

Birds and mammals living in the arctic tundra have another adaptive characteristic: they turn white during the winter, from the time the snow begins to fall. This change of color reduces the loss of heat and also helps the animals to blend in with their habitat until they are almost invisible. The ermine, the fox, and the arctic hare are champion artists of the quick change. In fact, the ermine's fur, which in the warmer weather is a reddish brown, becomes thick and white as soon as the first snow appears. Poor fellow, the tip of his tail remains dark, and so he can still be spotted, and so often loses his whole coat!

The tundra reindeer and his American neighbor, the caribou, are perhaps the only cud-chewing animals who are completely at home in the polar regions. They lumber around after the Lapps. Actually,

We might call the reindeer "queen of the tundra", since her kingdom is so enormous. This fabulous animal lives in the vast territories that surround the North Pole: Canada, Alaska, Greenland, Lapland and Siberia. The reindeer eats mostly lichen or reindeer moss, wild mushrooms and willow leaves. She is patient about finding exactly the daily fare she wants.

the Lapp shepherds are nomads because the reindeer herds must be continually on the move in search of pasture. They are on the lookout for northern lichen, also called reindeer moss, which the animals dig out with sharp cloven hooves. If this moss cannot be found, the reindeer will eat wild mushrooms and willow leaves. When the animal is successful in the search for food, the Lapp is happy, for to him the reindeer is everything. Everything about the reindeer is of use: his fur for mattresses; his skin for jackets, gloves, and pants; his nerves for thread to sew together the sealskin canoe (the thread expands upon contact with the water, and the seams are then waterproofed).

So let's catch the first sleigh that comes along, and go . . . where? You'll see when we turn the page.

A MOUNTAIN PEAK IS HOME

Whoever loves me will follow me! Clear the way! Hey I'm talking to you, boys and girls. Sorry if I've changed the subject abruptly, but you can understand my position. If I loosen my grip, goodbye. Oh, I forgot . . . see how confused I am. If you want to come with me, grab hold of one of these antennas . . . I mean antlers. You can trust him; he is one of the bold, the daring, the acrobatic ibex.

There: what we are looking at down there below us is "alpine country." But don't think that because I said alpine it means we are in the Alps. All regions above the altitude where trees grow are known as alpine—all over the world. Above this altitude begins the kingdom of eternal snow and glaciers. Below this, where trees and forests do grow, the animal life is similar to that found in the wooded areas of the plains. And the strip of land dividing the tree-growing regions with that of perpetual snow and ice can in turn be divided into two: a bush zone, and a zone where vegetation is sparse but grass more or less abundant. This subdivision is valid only in the highest mountain ranges. But we must remember that the topmost limit of the tree line depends upon latitude and upon the mountain slope itself—clearly it makes a difference which way it faces, north or south—and upon the type of climate.

Let us take an example to understand this more clearly. In Tibet the forests reach 15,000 feet, though the alpine zone on the southern slopes of the mountains there, the Himalayas, begins at 1,110 feet. In the Andes in the South American country of Colombia the forests begin at 9,000 feet. This is quite unlike the arctic regions of Norway. There, beyond the polar areas, this zone begins at 800 feet or less above sea level!

One can say generally that the characteristics of the alpine zones are due to their altitude above sea level, which causes a reduction in air pressure and temperature and an increase in humidity.

Vertebrates (all creatures with a spinal column) have different resistance levels to reductions in atmospheric pressure. For example, a man or a monkey begins to suffer from the altitude when barometric pressure is lower than 350 millibars. But a frog can hold out even at 100 millibars.

Oh dear! Sorry about all that scientific 71

The ibex, or wild goat (capra hibex) is an ancient animal. It is said that it originated in the Caucasus (in the south of Russia) and arrived on the Alps some million years ago. Once lord of high European peaks, today the ibex is forced to live in a herd of a few thousand among the crags and glaciers of the Gran Paradiso National Park (in northern Italy), and in some regions of Switzerland and Austria.

June

September

January

THE GROWTH OF ANTLERS

Among animals belonging to the deer family, adult males are recognized by horns which become great antlers that grow like branches of a tree. In the white tailed deer, they reach maximum growth by the November mating season. During this time, the male sheds the velvety covering of his antlers, so that he can use them as a sharp weapon along with his strong hooves, against rivals.

2 years

6 years

12 years

THE GROWTH OF HORNS

The Rocky Mountain sheep, is one of the wild sheep in the United States today. The horns are big: up to 1½ feet in the adult—the reason the animal is also known as "Big Horn". These horns appear at eight weeks, and look like hard little buttons. They grow rapidly during the second year, and every year after that a growth ring is added. In the other older rams, the tips of the horns curve back.

stuff. but I thought you needed to catch your breath. This matter of pressure is really quite a headache, but the concept is not too difficult to understand. To help you catch on, I waylaid Ludwig Von Drake by his coattail one day (he was in a hurry and didn't want to help) and now I'm passing on to you what he told me.

Air is thickest, or most dense, in low ground. As we go up a mountainside, the air gets thinner and thinner. Because all living things need the oxygen that air contains, there is not as much life found in the higher places of the earth. When men try to reach a towering mountain peak they must carry a supply of oxygen with

them. The climbers of Mount Everest (29,028 feet above sea level) carried an artificial oxygen tank as a necessary part of their pack. Others have been able to climb 27,000 feet without this aid. In Tibet and the Andes the highest permanent colony of man is at 17,000 feet. Shepherds and their flocks, however, frequently go as high as 18,000 feet. Mammals such as wild sheep and goats, yaks, hares and wolves live at high altitudes on the Asian mountains quite comfortably. The takin, too, which is a strange Tibetan antelope, lives on the high mountain peaks.

What's that, my friend? You want to   73

(left) A grey squirrel. This excellent climber builds his nest high up in trees, storing his nuts in the hollow trunks.

(below) A pretty fawn, completely motionless, blends in perfectly with the forest undergrowth, thanks to the spotted markings of his fur. All fawns have spotted fur.

(above) The chinchilla originated
in South America, but his thick,
soft, highly prized fur makes him
the victim of hunters.
A grey Arctic wolf
(at right).

know what sort of animal this *takin* is? Well, it's simple. It's a budorca. The budorca or takin is a cud-chewing animal living in the Himalayas who roams around a backyard some 6,500 feet to 16,000 feet in height. He doesn't suffer mountain sickness or vertigo (dizziness) and he's a fine jumper. The minute he scents danger, he swiftly leaps away to hide in some inaccessible cranny or mountain crag. He's very big; let's say he's a large, wild, shy sort of sheep. He does have a reputation for aggressiveness, spread around by no less a person than Marco Polo. This world traveller said that the takin was a ferocious beast who was always ready to attack the unwary traveler. He attacks all right, but his object is bamboo, which is his favorite food.

Perhaps you've noticed that I've already mentioned the scent of danger. That is because the four-legged alpine creatures, like other animals, have an incredible and indispensable sense of smell. With it they are able to detect danger. You must have noticed that the higher we go, the lower it gets. By that I mean this: the higher one goes the lower the temperature gets. In the Alps, it falls about one degree every 450 feet; in the Caucasus every 500 feet; and in the Andes every 550 feet. Ever-present glaciers and short warm periods virtually limit the alpine zones to two seasons: summer and winter. The second is very long, and the first definitely short. On the Italian Alps, for example, at an altitude of over 10,000 feet, average temperatures of above zero are registered during only two months of the year. The mountains, too, are often wrapped in fog and clouds, and this is a clear indication of the great humidity in the region.

The giant panda or bamboo bear is differentiated from other bears by a short muzzle, fur on the soles of his feet, and above all by the thick, rough fur divided into black and white areas. Barbary sheep (below), who live in the mountains of the Sahara, are clever at eluding hunters.

HOT AND COLD

The temperature drops as the altitude rises. This divides the vegetation and therefore the animal life, into zones. This is clearly shown by the varying kinds of land squirrels we meet as we climb up the mountains of the American Sierra Nevada. Every region has its Chip an' Dales! That's only a manner of speaking, for it is not applicable to all mammals. The attractive panda, you see, is only to be found—well-hidden—in the bamboo forests of Tibet above an altitude of 6,500 feet.

All right, boys and girls, you don't need to make faces at me. I'm not going off into some long scientific discussion. I know you want to hear more about the panda.

THE BLACK AND WHITE TEDDY BEAR

Black and white cat's feet! Now don't worry, I'm still talking about the panda. "Black and white cat's feet" is the translation of *ailuropoda melanoleucus*, the

Greek name for the giant panda. It is also called the bamboo bear, and Father David's bear. This animal, shy by nature, lives, as I have said before, in the bamboo forests on the high mountains of eastern Tibet and southern China. It has always been extremely rare and little known. Discovered in 1869 by the French naturalist and missionary Arnaud David (so that's why Father David's bear!) was only recently imported to Europe and America. The only living specimens in captivity are so few you can count them on your fingers. Except for the pandas in the Peking zoo, no panda in captivity has reproduced. We think of this attractive animal as a kind of black and white teddy bear. At least, I do. But it really is only a distant relative of the bear, and belongs in fact to the raccoon family. Whether because of his rarity, or his attractive appearance, the panda has been chosen as the symbol of the largest existing organization for wildlife conservation—the World Wildlife Fund. Discovered a century ago, it was not until about ten years ago that the panda was introduced into Europe. Before that he was known only on picture

post cards or fur coats. In 1939 a hunter took four live pandas out of their natural habitat and transported them to London. There's a story connected with that. You see, pandas eat chiefly bamboo shoots. Yes, I said *shoots*. Well, the London zoo, being fresh out of bamboo shoots at the moment, ordered all its most highly qualified specialists in charge of pandas to come up with—yes, a satisfactory menu. After a few sleepless nights pouring over their books (perhaps their cookbooks?) they finally thought of boiling carrots and serving them to the panda on a plate of bamboo leaves. The pandas were fooled, ate happily, and the problem was solved.

The golden panda is also very fond of bamboo shoots. This animal is sometimes called the cat bear, because he looks like a small bear and acts like a big cat!

LIVING WAY UP

The roughness of the land, the steepness of the mountain slopes, the canyons dug out by the dizzy, rapid mountain torrents and waterfalls, all favor those animals who are mountain climbers. The mountains are the realm of the ibex and wild mountain goat, the mouflon and the chamois. There are rodents, too, such as the marmot in the Alps and the chinchilla in Andes, who are inhabitants of the mountains.

Because only a few animals are able to survive in high altitude regions, there is a great similarity among those living in mountain ranges found in different parts of the earth. The animals living on the highest peaks of the islands of Java or the Philippines are similar to those found on the mountains of central Asia or North Africa. Let's look at someone climbing to meet us. He is a maned sheep, an animal characteristic of the mountains in the desert strip of North Africa. The male has long curved antlers, and no mane (in spite

of his name!) but a thick beard which reaches the ground. All of these sheep are excellent jumpers and climbers. Once they lived in large herds, and specialists believe they are a link between goats and sheep. Today, because of too many greedy hunters, the maned sheep is rare. The Egyptian sub-species is already extinct—this means it has died out—and the same fate awaits the others unless indiscriminate hunting is stopped. Fortunately, maned sheep do live safely in North Africa, and now have been introduced in other regions of the world, such as Canada and California, where they are well protected by rules and regulations.

THE GREAT JUMPERS

The animals of the mountain are jumpers in every sense of the word. They skip, too, and not only along a mountain path, but skip meals as well. Sorry for the pun . . . but it is really amazing that they can survive on so little food. The Himalayan yak, for example, is content with pasture land so sparse that domestic cattle would die of malnutrition if they had to live on

The mountain goat (above) lives in the mountains of North America. His thick, white fur makes him look quite dumpy and round. The alpine groundhog lives at an altitude of 4500 feet. He is very cautious and able to hear sounds at a great distance and this enables him to escape danger. (right) Snow leopard or irbis. Only a few hundred remain, living in the Himalayan mountains and other parts of Asia at an altitude between 6000 feet and 9000 feet. Its hairy tail of about 3 feet in length is almost as long as the rest of its body.

it. Bad weather often forces many mountain animals to migrate periodically into the valleys. The ibex, which in summer lives on the high peaks of the Gran Paradiso, must descend below the tree line in the winter to find his food. As I told you at the beginning of this chapter, I have one here within reach, and I'll tell you about him before he leaves us.

Master of the rocks and ravine, the extraordinary ibex has no equal when it comes to agility. He is able to jump across a distance of 24 or 30 feet with the greatest of ease, and over a void—that is, with nothing under him but an empty abyss! Imagine this male jumper weighs around 220 pounds! That, of course, is the weight of the adult male ibex (the young are like little puffs of cream-colored fur weighing only about 5 pounds). His horns, about 3 feet in length, weigh about 33 pounds.

Some years ago, this unusual animal was on the way to dying out. By this time you can guess who was responsible. Happily for them—and for us—a few wise men decided to protect them by creating a natural habitat where hunting was and still is forbidden.

Sorry, boys and girls, sometimes I can't help showing the sentimental side of my nature. I do love animals. Believe it or not, this is not only because I happen to be one of them. I believe firmly that all that lives should be respected: both to maintain the balance of nature, and also for the good of man himself. At this moment I'm thinking of someone, one of the greatest scientists the world has ever known, Albert Schweitzer. He can express it far better than I. At the end of each tiring day spent among the suffering, Dr. Schweitzer closed his prayers with these words: Protect and bless all living things; defend them from evil and let them sleep in peace.

IN SNOW AND ICE

Polar regions, here I come. Yes, friends, it's still me, Donald Duck. You'll have to take my word for it, because you can't see me. I'm shut up in an igloo.

No, that won't do, the editors tell me. I can't open up a chapter by being shut up. So out I come, through the window. It's on the ground floor, so I didn't hurt myself.

But I've already explored a bit up here at the pole, about four slides and seven headlong falls, by my count. But I've really prepared a great program for us, so let's make a start. First, of course, we must take our usual survey of the surroundings.

In many ways, living conditions at the poles are similar to those in the high mountains. The average daily and yearly temperatures fall regularly the more you climb and the closer you get to the poles. Here, the drop in temperatures means that precipitation is almost exclusively in the form of falling snow, which accumulates and makes the region prone to glaciers. Short summers are followed by long winters, just as in the mountain regions.

Around the poles, even those zones at sea level remain almost constantly covered by snow and ice. On the other hand, where the sun isn't hidden by fog and where the snow is almost always blown away by the wind, the ground warms up. Then the coat of ice which covers it disappears and, at least for a short time, we are able to study the relatively favorable living conditions.

POLES APART

The Arctic polar regions are those surrounding the North Pole. They are "all ice", it is generally believed.

The Antarctic regions are those around the South Pole, where the penguins are. That should help you remember which is which! If you follow me for a bit, you'll learn some more, my friends. First of all, the big difference between the two polar regions is that a great land mass is to be found in Antarctica only. In fact we talk of the South Pole as the Antarctic continent—while the North Pole is a mass of frozen water.

In Antarctica, the winters are not as cold as at the North Pole, although summers are decidedly colder. Because summer temperatures always remain below that necessary for the growth of vegetation, in Antarctica we find only two flowering plants and few kinds of moss and algae. Vertebrates do not live at the center of the South Pole: birds, particularly the penguins, and mammals that are found mostly on the coasts, find their food in the sea and are therefore dependent on it for survival.

Even the invertebrates are scarce in this part of the world and we can say that there are no animals far from the penguin colonies. There, after some searching, it is

possible to come across a few primitive insects such as wingless flies, some acari and very few protozoa. These tiny inhabitants of Antarctica live actively for a few days of the year only, and spend the rest of their lives (sometimes even years) half frozen, in a state of semi-sleep. The only mammals that come regularly to the coast of Antarctica to reproduce are certain species of seal. But at this point, stop! With the editors' permission, I believe I'll have a swim. Anyone join me for a lesson? I'm going to a special school—run by seals.

SCHOOL FOR SEALS

A newborn seal faces one problem right away. He is an animal whose only hope of survival (he eats fish) and defense (his

(above) The sharp pointed snout of a young otter. (below) A Greenland seal pup, still covered by the thick white fur which makes him the target of bloody hunts. He is anxiously waiting for his mother, whose dark head is emerging from a hole in the ice. Greenland seals are sea-going and migratory. They'd rather live on floating icebergs than on land.

best defense is escape) lies in the sea. So guess what he must do, first thing?

The answer is, you say, that he must learn to swim. How obvious: well, yes, but try telling that to the baby seals. The water is cold when they are told to go in and they all set up a tremendous squeal. Mother seal knows that one is born able to swim. Since for seals it is a matter of necessity, she tries first of all to encourage her young to follow her into the water. If they don't, well, she knocks them in with her fin. Then she dives quickly after them and swims back and forth and around them, ready to come to their help if needed.

THE SEAL AND HIS COUSINS

The word "seal" is a general heading for three groups of water mammals: the true seal and sea elephant; the otter and sea lion; and the walrus. In spite of their excellent swimming ability, all of these mammals can sometimes move with great agility on the land. Males of all the species have a belligerent temper. They must protect a large number of wives and children and so they take for themselves part of the coastline. No rival is permitted to approach this area and the male seal tries to keep them off with ferocious screams. If, however, another male approaches unafraid, the defender male will fight until the last drop of blood has been shed. All members of the seal family have a strong feeling for the family and they live in herds, especially during mating season.

Other mammals found only at the North Pole are the musk ox and the polar bear. The polar bear, or white bear, lives for most of the year on the Arctic Ocean ice pack. His daily menu features certain local specialties such as various kinds of seal. But during the summer the polar bear must, because of the breaking of the ice, find shelter on land where he is forced to be content with whatever he can find in the way of food. Usually this is roots and berries. Sometimes polar bears will ransack the eskimo's reserves. The domain of the polar bear, we can see, is restricted to regions where he can have solid ground under foot as much as possible. Usually, the bear cubs are born in March or April

A colony of sea lions photographed on the coast of the Pribilof Island in the Baltic Sea. The fur of these animals is valuable. At the beginning of the mating season the males reach the island by May, following long and complicated routes and relying on their fantastic sense of direction. They are joined by their females in mid-June. (right) Some sea lions: The male differs from the female (top) in his enormous size and thick moustache. The pups (center) are born between August and December and are cared for by the mother.

after the female has retreated into a den.

It does seem strange that this animal, that lives so far from human settlements, is on the verge of dying out. It was a long time ago, around 1600, when the decline of the polar bear population began. This was when ships began to ply back and forth in Arctic waters. As whale hunting became less profitable, merchant fleets devoted their time to capturing seals. This led in turn to the hunting of polar bears. Up to that time, only the eskimo had killed the bear, and this only when it was a matter of survival. Their hunting had but little impact on the population of this animal. For centuries the desolate polar regions had provided safe refuge for the white bear (polar bear, remember?). But with the introduction of fire arms, and an increase in modern means of transportation, including the airplane, the survival of this unique species of mammal is seriously threatened. Then the fact that

These two pages show the Polar bear, one of the largest carnivorous animals in the world.

A herd of walrus, (above) with their characteristic long tusks, basking in the coastal sun.

he lives outside the territorial waters, in what one might call a rather damp "no man's land" makes control over hunting and trapping enormously difficult if not outright impossible.

In 1965, at Fairbanks, Alaska, the first national conference on polar bears was held. Its purpose was the studying of a plan that would offer the interested nations (the U.S., Soviet Russia, Canada, Norway and Denmark) a means of guaranteeing the polar bear's survival. Agreement was reached. This encouraged scientific research on the life cycle of the polar bear, research necessary for enacting a plan to permit hunting while preventing the dying out of the animal.

The same international guarantee protects the survival of another arctic mammal: the walrus. This distinct relative of the seal is sometimes as long as 12 feet and weighs sometimes as much as 2,600 pounds. The females are smaller than the males, whose tusks are sometimes as long as 3¼ feet. The walrus uses his front tusks to dig and find mollusks—his chief food—as well as for fighting and to defend himself.

Walruses usually live in large mixed herds of a thousand or more, on small islands, along the rocky coasts or on floating icebergs.

A Canadian law of 1931 restricted the hunting of the walrus to eskimos and the few whites living in the region. This law also forbade export of the animal's skin and ivory tusks in their natural states. Further restrictions governing hunting were enacted in 1949. Under these only a few head could be killed each year. Walruses are also well protected under Danish and Norwegian law. In Soviet Russia walrus hunting is restricted to Eskimos and ciukci. Today the walrus has a better life. This shows that good will and the joint efforts of different peoples can encourage the enjoyment (and use) of natural resources without destroying them.

A CLEVER DEFENDER

Coming towards us with a measured pace and looking almost totally indifferent to everything around him, is the musk ox. He has the appearance of knowing a thing or two, and above all, of being extremely sure of himself. The musk ox, or musky . . . of all the herbivores (plant-eating animals) in the Arctic, ranges the farthest north. He is really a living legend, a survivor of the ice age. And we see him today just as he appeared to the painters of the prehistoric stone age. The musk ox species has been able to survive long centuries of polar climate thanks to the protection of his extremely thick fur. And he has always managed to resist the attacks by wolves because of very clear defense strategy: as soon as their enemy is sighted or scented on the horizon, the musk oxen join ranks and form a square. In the center are the females and offspring; the males form the outer ranks, their horns pointed out and ready to strike.

If the wolves have any sense at all, they'll act as though they see nothing and go on about their business. If they insist —well, they'll lose their skins. The poor musk ox often loses his skin too, poor fellow, when he is confronted by man.

THE ESKIMO'S BEST FRIEND

Hey, my friends, pinch me quick. Ow . . . don't let's exaggerate, now. I just wanted to see if I was awake or dreaming. Just look down there, will you? Aren't those a bunch of dogs racing towards us at full speed? Hey, you there! No, boys and girls, I don't mean you, I'm talking to the dogs here.

The fur of polar animals not only changes color with seasonal weather changes but may sometimes— as in the case of the arctic fox pup shown above, puff up to keep him warm in the snow, thanks to a thick, insulating layer of air.

What dears they are and so obedient! They haven't moved an inch. Ah, there, show me your identification: Siberian Husky. Height: 2 feet. Color of fur: light or dark brown. Profession? Sleigh pullers. Residence? North Pole. Distinguishing features: one dried fish daily on average, between the teeth, and two bright blue eyes.

Well, my friends and readers: I've just introduced you to the fantastic husky. This is the marvelous Eskimo dog, so generous and faithful that he will risk his own life for his master. He is the famous four-legged friend of the men who live at the Pole, who works for him and almost never tires.

It is no coincidence that the huskies are sticking their muzzles into this chapter on bears. Why? Because they know that the Eskimo fur traders and diggers for gold could never survive without them in these polar regions. Eskimo dog, or sleigh dog, are vague terms, and we can do better than that. Actually, there are four main kinds of dogs who pull sleighs: the Samoyede, the Alaskan Malamute, the Greenlander, and the Siberian husky, which is the smallest and the fastest. The Samoyede, with its double coat of white, cream or light tan-colored fur, has been pure bred for a very long time. Originally they were the companions of the nomads who roamed the Siberian tundra. Then they were used for herding reindeer, hunting bear, and pulling sleighs. They were so highly regarded that they slept in their owners' tents as members of the family. Today, many of these four-legged friends have been replaced by more powerful mechanical means of transportation.

90

THEY LIVE IN WATER BUT NEED AIR

Unexpectedly, friends (how's that for an opener?). Well, as I was saying, unexpectedly, in this chapter I was handed the enormous job of telling you all about sea mammals. There is hardly space enough here to tell you about such a vast matter. No sooner am I started than I'm getting my line all tangled! I'll cut it, and this unnecessary chatter as well, and begin.

The only mammals that are completely adapted to under-water living—in fact they are not able to exist outside of water—are the cetacean. That is, the whales and dolphins. They are mammals whose bodies have undergone outstanding evolutionary changes: their front legs have become fins and their rear legs completely disappeared. The tail has become a flat, horizontal fin used to propel them through the water. They also have a rear fin, called the dorsal fin, of fatty tissue which while it has nothing to do with a fish dorsal, does serve to show the similarity between fish and cetacean.

This resemblance deceived man for centuries. Whales and dolphins were considered fish, even though it was known that many of them were furry! It was even more of an error since they did know that whales and dolphins breast fed their young. It wasn't until the 17th century that the great English naturalist John Ray classified these "animals" as mammals. That these species originated from land forms there is no doubt. The development can be seen when the species is the embryo. Then, their jaws begin to grow, as in all mammals. As the fetus develops, the front paws become pectoral fins and the rear ones disappear. The nostrils, appearing earlier on the front of the snout as in all mammals, gradually move towards the top of the head and become the famous "air holes."

A WHALE OF AN ANIMAL

Like other mammals, cetaceans must breath air, because they have lungs and not gills. The well-known water spout of the whale and sperm whale, for example, is nothing more than water vapor under pressure, exhaled from the lungs and expelled through the air holes when the animals surface to breathe. Their

93

capacity for remaining under water without breathing for long periods of time is legendary. This is possible, at least partly, because of their enormous lung capacity. A big whale can store more than 2114 quarts of air and because of his great oxygen reserve, is able to dive as deep as 1100 feet. Cases have been known of cetaceans which, to escape capture, have dived as deep as 3200 feet, where the water pressure is tremendous. Almost the entire body structure of the whale is relatively non-compressible, because the body's water content is about two thirds of the entire mass. This is so with all mammals, including man. The only part of the body structure of the whale which can be damaged by strong pressure are the lungs, which in cetaceans, may be reduced to one tenth of the original volume. Although it seems a contradiction, it is due to these mechanical obstacles that the cetaceans, which dive to great depths, have lungs weighing less and with half the capacity of land mammals of comparable proportion. On the other hand, dolphins, which do not dive very deep, have lungs that are proportionately about double the size of those of land mammals. In fact, of the air breathed in, it is the oxygen dispersed into body tissue which counts. In cetaceans, only 9% of the oxygen inhaled is retained by the lungs; more than 40% is stored in the muscles and another 40% in the blood. This explains why the lung volume, to reduce effects of pressure, can decrease to one tenth of its original volume. The amount of energy its body is able to generate without utilizing oxygen accounts for the cetacean's ability for deep diving. Here is another interest-

94

ing point: more body heat is dispersed in water than in air; therefore warm-blooded animals must reduce this thermic dispersion in one way or another. Our cetaceans have solved this problem by means of a thick layer of fat that serves as insulation. In the whale, this layer is 1½-2 feet thick!

Man has hunted the cetaceans for commercial profit since ancient times. But it wasn't until the sixteenth century voyages of European explorers who ventured toward the Arctic seas in search of routes to the Orient that whales were really in

The killer whale (left) one of the cetacean family, lives in chilly waters. He is a greedy, swift predator whose savagery is greater than the shark. The killer whale is not afraid to attack a whale larger than he. His head is very small compared to the rest of his body, but his mouth has from 40-56 teeth—his most deadly weapon.

danger. On their way the voyagers came across large schools of cetaceans, and from that time on whaling fleets were formed to hunt them. These fleets became more and more efficient and destructive, pitilessly slaughtering these peaceful, unorganized but extraordinary lords of the seas. So thorough was this wholesale killing that today some species, such as the blue whale, are virtually extinct. The existence of all of them is seriously threatened. In spite of the efforts of an international commission with eighteen member nations, which has established severe restrictions on hunting, it is not possible to tell whether these gigantic sea mammals will survive for future generations.

A BIG FAMILY

The cetaceans are divided into two groups. The first Mysticeti, includes whales and rorquals (12 species in all, including the red whale and fin back).

Whales and rorquals have no teeth but a peculiar set of blades called whalebones. These hang from the palate of the mouth and filter the small shellfish which are the main food of these cetaceans.

Among the largest of the species, and almost extinct, is the blue rorqual. It is 60 feet in length and weighs some 50 tons—a little bit like twenty-five elephants put together!

In fact, it is the largest animal that has ever existed on the earth. The dinosaur pales by comparison, a lightweight of a few tons only!

The second group of cetaceans are the Odontocetans. These mammals are equipped with teeth, and feed on fish and relatively large prey. The group includes species often differing with one another: the sperm whale, the zifi, dolphins, globicephales, the beluga, narwhal, the killer whale, the Amazon River Inia, the Ganges dolphin, and the very rare Chinese lake dolphin found only in the Tungting lake in Hunan province.

The elegant pirouette of the ballerina whale, or Megaptera. (above) These members of the cetaceans *live in large schools. Next to him is the black* Globicephalus, *or pilot whale. The* marwhal, the *only* cetacean *with a long tooth, shaped like a sword.*

One of the most curious of all cetaceans is the narwhal, found only in the
Arctic seas between Alaska, around
Greenland to Siberia. Full-grown nar-
whals have but two teeth horizontally
placed in the jaw. In the male the left-
hand one grows to become a serated tusk
sometimes 9 feet in length. No one knows
what this tusk is for, and the fact that
only the male has it refutes the theory
that it serves to spear prey or to break
the ice after surfacing, to breath.

The killer whale, the most terrifying
monster of the seas, actually is a member
of the dolphin family; they are to be
found all over the world. Males are often
27 feet long. The killer whale has an
impressive set of teeth, which allow it to
feed not only on fish like other dolphins,
but on birds and sea mammals as well. It
savagely attacks seals, otters, and even
other whales and rorquals without hesita-
tion.

But in spite of their unusual savagery,

killer whales are rather docile when in captivity, and even make friends with man. One killer whale in Seattle's aquarium even allowed visitors to ride on its back, and seemed to enjoy giving them a ride.

When it comes to the question of intelligence, however, it is the dolphin who is by far the most interesting of the cetaceans. Their brain, believe it or not, has more convolutions than man's. It is amazing how many tricks the dolphin is able to learn with no trouble at all. We may even say they enjoy learning them. Many of the incredible tales of the dolphin's ability must be true. It has been proved that they really have rescued men from drowning. We are able to believe this when we learn that the dolphins help their own sick or wounded companions by lifting them up out of the water so that their nostrils reach the surface and permit them to breath.

Very recently studies have confirmed the ability of the dolphin to imitate human speech, even though their version is so fast that we are only able to distinguish the words by means of special instruments.

Before I forget, I'd like to point out one more interesting piece of information.

Dolphins and other large cetaceans, such as sharks, are often escorted by schools of pilot fish. These are small fish which often follow larger ones around (and sometimes even ships) in the hopes of picking up a meal from their leftovers.

I told you, boys and girls, that our visit to the whales and dolphins would be worth it. And now the night is about to cover everything with its dark blue velvet cape studded with stars. But we can't sleep yet. There is a new voyage ahead of us, an unusual one, to see the mammals of the air.

A school of dolphins. These cetaceans (who have 260 teeth!) show unusual ability for communicating among themselves and also have a high level of intelligence. Other qualities of the dolphin are sturdiness, agility, sociability and affection for offspring.

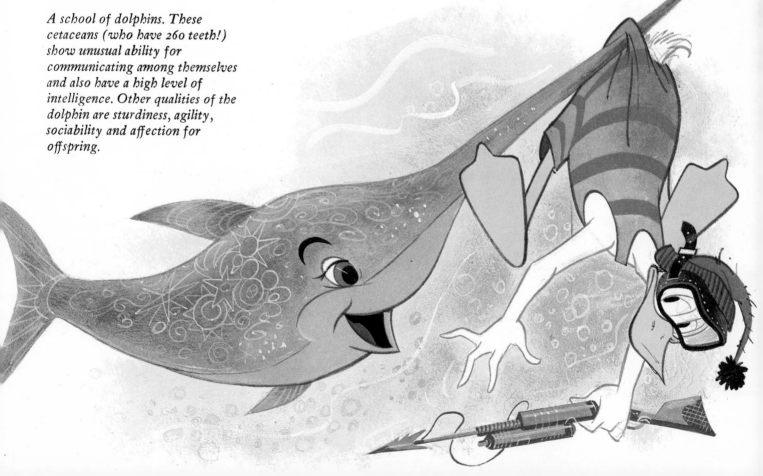

THEY WHO SEE BEST IN THE DARK

What can I say, my friends? How can I begin, when I know perfectly well that as soon as you turn the page you'll jump out of your skins? I took a look myself and believe me, I hit the ceiling. I feel sure, however, that once you've read a paragraph or two, you will be fascinated by these interesting little mammals. They are particularly useful to agriculture and to the balance of nature, and so are protected by law. Let me proceed at once then, with the introductions.

Here are the bats, the only mammals who have effectively conquered the world of the air (how about us?) and fly. Their bodies have undergone structural changes so that they can do this. The front legs, with highly developed "fingers," except for the thumb, support the wing membrane. This membrane is made of a thin, elastic skin, which is webbed and connects front legs, rear legs, and tail. The rear fingers are free, allowing the bats to cling to branches and other objects in their characteristic upside down position.

The chest muscles of this flying mammal are particularly well developed, so that the bat can move its wings in a somewhat different fashion than the bird. Actually, the wing moves up and down, and round about as well, in a circular fashion. The frequency of wing movement varies according to wing size: the "flying fox" moves his wings slowly and calmly; the common bat much more rapidly.

The common or garden night bat is able to fly as fast as 30 mph. The so-called rat-eared bat, with his wilder and more rounded wings, is not able to exceed 10 mph. Some of the smaller kinds of bat have more agility than birds, with the possible exception of the hummingbird. Like the hummingbird, these bats eat flowers, and are able to glide or remain still in the air, over the same spot. The larger type of bat, on the other hand, takes advantage of ascending air currents, flying with outspread wings with the same ease as the sea gull or hovering predatory bird. Wings closed, bats are able to climb and run on land, just like other four-legged animals and with far greater ease than we might expect. There are even running bats!

FLYING BY EAR

Among the fossils that have been dug up after being buried for many centuries, are perfectly formed specimens of bats that date back over 50,000,000 years. Here is proof of the evolutionary success of the bat, a mammal which has shared the kingdom of the air with birds since time immemorial. Thanks to their ease of movement, they are to be found all over the world except at the poles and in the deserts. In these regions they are unable to find the flying insects on which they live.

In the dark world inhabited by nearly all kinds of bats, sight is certainly not tremendously important. On the other hand, it is clear that in order to capture the very swift insects on which they feed, they must have a capacity for, and sureness in flying that is exceptional. It was the great Italian doctor and naturalist, Lazzaro Spallanzani who first (1765) discovered which of their senses was used by bats for night flying. In an experiment, he strung threads all across a room and let the bats fly freely. He noticed that their flight was calm, and that they avoided the taut-strung threads easily. He noted also that even with their eyelids sealed shut they had no trouble. Greatly surprised and excited, Spallanzani continued his experiments, and found that the bats literally bumped into one another and into the threads when their ears were sealed! The scientist concluded from this, that the sense of hearing is more important to a bat in flight than his sense of touch or sight. As so often happens, in the time in which he lived, few people took Spallanzani seriously, and his experiments were largely ignored.

ANIMAL RADAR

It was only many years later that a Dutchman and an American, working independently and using the most modern techniques, were able to prove that bats emit high frequency sounds. These sounds are not heard by the human ear. But as they bounce off various objects the sounds are heard by bats. This "bouncing" of sound waves is the principle of radar. The scientists merely applied to radio equipment the system which nature had been using for millions of years. The sound waves, also known as "ultra sounds," or high frequency vibrations, were emitted through the bats' mouths. When the sound hit an obstacle, they bounced back and were picked up by the bats' sensitive ears. The bat judges the distance between himself and the object by the time it takes for the sound to bounce back.

Many bats, such as the "horseshoe bat" or the "vampire" bat, have straight membranes on their noses. For many years scientists were unaware of the function of these membranes. Then they discovered a connection between the larynx and the nasal cavity. They realized that the membranes acted as frequency modulators for ultra sonic noise vibrations which the bats are able to emit even with their

A bat (right) prepares for the night, hanging by his feet and folding his wings. A talented flyer, he can go as far as 62 miles from home batting his wings 16-20 times a second.

mouths closed. Furthermore, because they hunt their prey in the dark, they often catch small objects or insects which are poisonous. To avoid this, they put into use a sort of second nose. Bats are social animals who live often in large colonies in caves, old buildings, and in the trunks of large trees. One of the most famous group of caves in the world, the Carlsbad Caverns in New Mexico, is home to at least 9 million Tadarida bats.

HAVE A BALL WITH A BAT

With ainmals as sociable as these, there has to be a domestic variety, or one that permits taming. This is the "flying fox," which lives on fruit rather than insects. There are many kinds of this species: the largest, also called the Kalong, has a wing spread of 5 feet. If you decide that you want a bat in the house, don't pick one of these large ones. Choose one of his smaller brothers instead, one that you can easily find on sale. When you bring him home, give him a very large cage so that he can fly about in it with wings outspread. He wants a cage where he can climb and hang upsidedown in the daytime. In the evening, he needs freedom to fly about at will, and you must let him out of the cage. The bat is used to a very hectic night life, and if you force him to sit in a corner for too long, he'll die. How do you tame him? First of all, give him time to get used to his new home. Then pick him up, and feed him. Let him climb on your shoulders and over your clothes. Treat him carefully always, and avoid any quick movements, and you'll make friends soon enough. But protect your hands from

his bites with gloves. His favorite foods? The choice is a bit limited, because he likes only a few things. But they are good: milk, ripe fruit—grapes and ripe bananas especially—cooked apples and canned fruit. Take good care of your bat's health: avoid drafts and keep his corner in partial darkness, at a constant temperature not lower than 66°F.

And now, struck dumb at what I've revealed, and astonished at how much I've managed to learn about these strange mammals, I shall retreat. I am so overcome with emotion I'll have to leave you. Besides, I want to be the first to move into the next chapter.

(opposite) This Asian bat clearly doesn't find this upside down rest position at all tiring. Firmly clutching a branch with his rear claws, he not only sleeps but can also hibernate for months in the same place. (above) The bat was originally an insect eater, but to survive he sometimes settles for fruit and flower nectar, like the long-nosed bat shown here.

THE ANIMALS WHO LIVE WITH US

Perhaps I should have mentioned them before, I mean right at the beginning, when I introduced myself and told you I was to be your guide on this long, fascinating adventure-filled journey through the mammal world. I did think of it, really, but decided to keep this as an ace up my sleeve. But now, dear friends, the time has come to lay my cards on the table. This chapter is dedicated to the animals the whole world loves, those creatures who live close to you and for you.

But be patient with me for just another minute or two. I want to tell you a little bit about the famous Swedish naturalist Karl von Linne—or Carolus Linnaeus (the Latin form of his name) as he is generally called. We have mentioned his name before.

Linnaeus (1707-1778) conceived of a system for subdividing and classifying the plants and animals (from the time man began to notice the plant and animal life around him, no one except Aristotle had thought of cataloging this life according to the characteristics plants and animals had in common). The problem of classifications became even greater when stimulated by the voyages, explorations, conquests and discoveries of new worlds. Travelers, merchants and explorers continued to bring back word of plants and animals never seen before. Thousands and thousands of new forms of animal and vegetable life were added constantly to those already known. This naturally made for a great deal of confusion.

What was it that Linnaeus did? He thought up a very simple system. Thanks to his system, laymen and professional scientists of all nationalities are able to refer to one common name for any particular plant or animal—with no possibility of confusion or misunderstanding.

Linnaeus started off with a simple and ingenious plan: he gave every species two Latin names. The first indicated the genus to which the animal belonged, and the second indicated the species. The specific name is written with a small letter (lower case). This system is still in use, and is known as the binomial (two name) or Linnaean system. I'll explain it by taking an example: First of all, let's suppose we all come from different countries and therefore speak different languages. We understand only our own. Everything will be easier if we call everything under the Linnaean system—an animal will be called by its scientific Latin name. The generic name is written with a capital letter—Canic, Cervus, Equus. The specific name is written without a capital—porcinus, italiae, elaphus—to indicate the species. Throughout the world these two categories are fixed and immutable.

107

Well, that little side step took longer than I thought it would. But I think this clarification was necessary, even indispensable, for us, and a salute to the original-minded Swedish naturalist.

FROM HUNTER TO HERDSMAN

Now, boys and girls, is a good time to say "let's start from the beginning." That is, let us take a jump backwards in time together, to see what went on thousands and thousands of years ago.

Primitive man was a hunter. He picked berries and fruit when he found them. Certainly many tribes were nomadic, moving from place to place in search of the animals they hunted, or fleeing from the bad weather. When man made tools out of stones, he took the first steps on

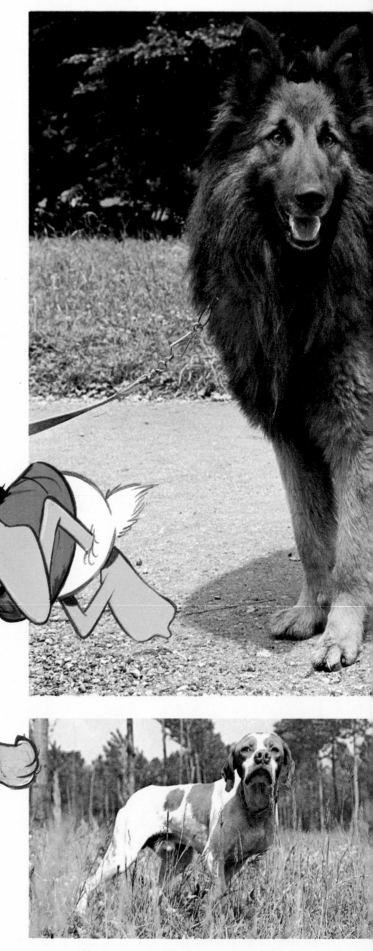

*(above, left) Belgian sheepdog, Tervueren variety.
The use of these and all other shepherd dogs
dates back to prehistoric times. The Belgian
shepherd belongs to the so-called wolfdog group.
(left, below) A pointer. These dogs have a highly
developed sense of smell and are used for hunting.
Above, right: Setter—a typical hunting dog famous
for his beauty and hunting skill, bred by the
English as early as 16th century. (below) Him is the
brindled Boxer, a close relative of the bulldog,
and one of the most recently pedigreed (1895).
He is considered a great friend of children. Below
him is the light colored German shepherd.*

the road to progress. These tools were
weapons and utensils crudely chopped
from rock. What was our caveman able
to do with these tools? The terms of the
problem were so simple that the solution
to it comes by itself. Primitive man was
trying to find the means to improve his
way of life in accordance with necessities
of the environment in which he lived.
And since he knew that plants and animals

were both necessary for his survival, man turned his attention to them.

THE FAITHFUL FRIEND

It is not possible to know for certain whether man first cultivated plants or tamed animals, because the development of a primitive sort of agriculture could have taken place without the immediate use of animals. But it is almost certain that the first friend of man was the dog, or rather, the forefather of most dogs that we know today: the jackal. Great packs of jackals gathered around the hunters' fires, in ancient times, waiting for leftovers to scavenge.

Konrad Lorenz, the well-known authority on animal behavior, tell us: "One of the most intelligent deeds of those prehistoric hunters was the deliberate tossing of a piece of meat to some fearless jackal roaming around, not far from the fire. This was the beginning of the eternal friendship between the dog and man". The jackal really is nothing more than a wild dog, rather more timid than the wolf. For this very reason, it is easier to tame him. To tell the truth, primitive man probably found it quite comforting to have the jackal following him around. Let me explain that. When the nomadic hunting tribes moved across open land, nightfall must have made the landscape more hostile and frightening than it was during the day. The excited barking of the jackals warned against any approaching danger, whether an animal or an enemy tribe.

At first, the relationship between man and this "near-dog" jackal must have been one of mutual assistance or reciprocal toleration. But when some female

pack-leader, rendered more courageous by knowledge that man was not a danger to her, was able to lead man to some wounded animal hiding in the underbrush, a new relationship was established. Of course, it probably didn't take place just exactly as we have described. But the fact remains that the first dogs were used by man for hunting. Only later were they used for defense. We can date the taming of dogs certainly back 10,000 years or more, because greyhounds as we know them today existed in Egypt in the 4th millenium B.C. The Afghan hound of

(*opposite, above*) *two giant schnauzers. These dogs are of German origin and love to travel. During the days of the horse and carriage, they ran between the horses legs, practically under their hooves.* (*opposite*) *A Dalmation, an excellent watchdog and highly prized for his black and white coat. He was once called a "carriage dog", and now sometimes a firehouse dog.* (*above, left*) *A chow chow, supposedly introduced into Europe from China in 1879. Next to him is a group of lively, intelligent cocker spaniels. The parade is closed by a basketful of white Persian kittens.*

today probably originated in Sinai, because it is mentioned more than once in an Egyptian scroll dated 40000 B.C. They are also pictured on a vase of the period. Legend has it that this was the breed of dog saved by Noah. The good old man, just before the Flood, took a couple of these hounds into the Ark. Another legend tells us that a leak sprung in the Ark and that these dogs stopped it up with their noses. This explains why their noses are always so cold and damp! Oh, just a moment. Malachi the Cat wants a word with us. What's that? Ah yes, of course, absolutely! Of all our animal friends, the one which knows best how to show its love for man is the dog. And if Malachi says it . . .

HOLY CATS

Not everyone will agree that the cat is really a domestic animal. Certain of the species were known and venerated in ancient Egypt in 1600 B.C. There seems little question that they originated from the wild African cat, and not from the wild European cat which even today is not easily tamed.

Well, boys and girls, don't believe that a mere flick of the tail disposes of all of Malachi's ancestors. I should say not. That little feline is too much a part of my daily life. If I didn't say more about that extraordinary, regal, and arrogant race to which he and fifty million other cats belong, I believe he'd be offended. In ancient Egypt, the cat was worshipped and protected by special laws. Anyone who dared offend their feline majesties was punished by death. Ulp! But to tell you the honest truth, this came about because the Egyptians, after taming the cat, had trained it to guard the warehouses of *(opposite) The tabby cat (Syrian or tiger cat) is the most common. While they are usually of grey and yellow stripes, they may also be beige, brown, dark grey, silver and blue in color. (opposite, below) Siamese cats, with tan fur, black mask, paws and tail, are very aggressive in spite of their sweet and bright blue eyes. (right) Przhevalski horse, plentiful on the steppes of Siberia and China. It is one of the untamed species of horse still left. (below) The graceful canter of a horse running free. Today even the so-called wild horses (like the famous mustangs, and the cimarrones of South America) are actually the descendents of domesticated horses returned to their wild state.*

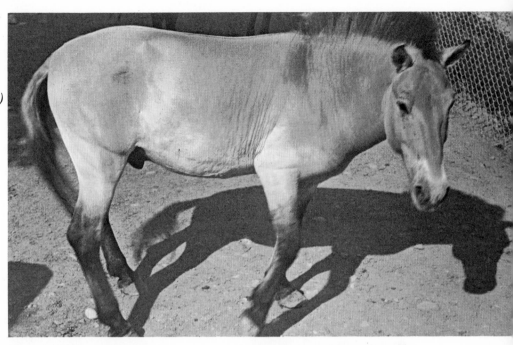

wheat against rats. Then, as the cats performed their duties well, they were considered sacred and were worshipped.

It must have been about then that our felines adopted their strange, aloof and slightly intellectual look. This was after they found out that Confucius had a favorite cat. To say nothing of Mohammed (567-632), and all his followers had a weakness for cats. In Japan during the same period cats were trained to guard the temples and defend the precious manuscripts kept there from enemy paws—I mean hands.

Cats were always kept on a leash. It was only in 1600 A.D. that an imperial decree allowed them to run free. But why? In one word: to catch the small rats which were ruining the silk industry.

Perhaps this explains why even today the Japanese hold cats in such high esteem. It seems—but don't let Malachi hear us—that the Japanese cat is the most spoiled in the world. Meow!

(left) A group of donkeys grazing—on the island of Asinara near Sardinia, in the Mediterranean. According to estimates, Italy and Spain are superior in the breeding of donkeys. This "friend of man" is highly important in regions which are arid and rough in terrain, and where agriculture is poor. (above) Horses of the fjords, resting. Famous throughout Norway for their strength, these horses are used for transportation in mountainous regions. Their hide is thicker than most, and this helps them bear the great cold. These horses of the fjords belong to a race of cart horses, so called because their bone structure is heavy, their trunk strong, the legs short and thick.

(far, left) The Andalusian mule. The mule is the son of a donkey and a female horse. It is a rather rough animal, well able to endure hardship and rough climate.

115

ON THE GRAZING LANDS

Let's leave his Majesty the Cat to his silks and laces, and go for a walk in the pastures to relax. Look, boys and girls, there's a piece of wool caught on a branch. Good enough. We're on the right path. We must be approaching the herd —of a family that is very important without whose cooperation man would never have survived.

Sheep, goats, oxen and pigs, like all other animals before they became part of

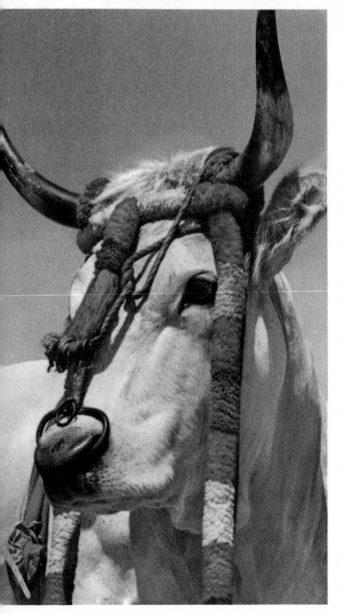

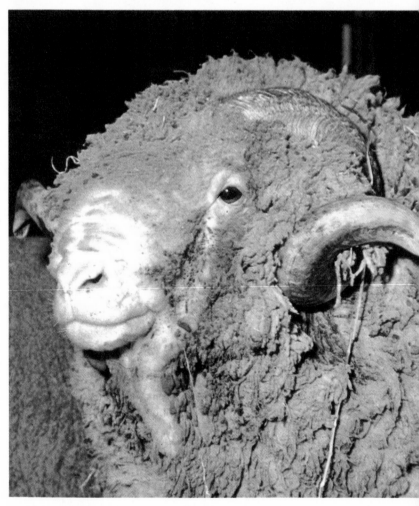

(top) The antelope's large dreamy eyes are particularly evident in this picture of a cub (lower, left) Splendid example of the Italian ox. (above) Australian ram of the famous Merino breed, with characteristic curved horns.

the world in which we live, were all wild. Wild and free, to roam endless pasture lands—this was their life before man came into the picture. Of course, they had seen man, through the eyes of preceding generations. But the one they came across now was very different from the others. This man had fire, some rough implements, a roof, and a family. He had intelligence and the means to make use of it. From that moment on, it was the end of freedom for the sheep, goats, pigs and oxen. No more wild racing through the boundless prairies.

(below) Black and white Dutch cattle, called Frisians. This breed was brought to the United States and has developed into the best milk giving cows in the world. In Holland, these cattle are the wealth of the country people and dairy owners, and they receive the best of care. For example, they are protected against cold morning mists by old blankets or jute covers. Their stalls are built according to scientific methods and the animals live in perfect hygienic conditions. Holsteins, as they are called in America, can produce up to 6800 quarts of milk in a year.

117

It is difficult to establish exactly when goats and sheep were tamed. The skeletons found near ancient settlements don't differ greatly from the wild species. As far as goats are concerned the difference between the wild and domestic animal lies inside the horns containing marrow—rounded in wild goats and flat in the domestic ones. Experts calculate that as far back as the 9th century B.C., goats were tamed by Iraqi tribes. Sheep were probably tamed around the same period and in a short time became more numerous than goats all over the Near East.

Pigs were also tamed quite early. We

(left) Sheep breeding in Europe generally is decreasing in the plains. In the mountain regions sheep breeding still represents a source of income, because many Alpine pastures are unfit for use by cattle. (above) Maremma oxen grazing.

do not know when the domestication of cattle took place. Certainly they were unknown to the ancient Egyptians before 3200 B.C.

HAVE A SEAT AND RIDE

An animal also very close to our hearts is the horse, and here he comes! Where can we find a more noble animal as far as bravery and looks are concerned? Where can we find an animal that has contributed more in the making of history, side by side with man?

All right, I can imagine what you are

(above) African oxen in a Masai village in Kenya. This animal is a cross between the Mediterranean ox and the zebu, which reached Africa (Egypt) from India about 4000 years ago. African cattle give very little milk (3-4 quarts per day) because of the poor pasture land on which they graze. (below) Bulls grazing, in Andalusia, Spain. These animals, reared in a semi-wild state, are the ones used for bull fighting.

trying to say. You're correct, too. All animals, from the smallest to the biggest, from the most handsome to the ugliest, from the gentlest to the most ferocious, all were indispensable fragments making up the marvelous mosaic of nature. So it would be only logical if we talked of all animals in the same way. But you have to agree that some animals are closer to our hearts than others.

Not much is known about when or how the donkey and the horse were tamed. Scientists tend to think that the horse was first used as a domestic animal on the Eurasian steppes between the Ukraine and Pakistan between 3000 and 2500 B.C. The Sumerians in Mesopotamia

(below) The white llama. The vicuna, the guanaco, and the llama all live in South America, though they belong to the camel family. The llama was domesticated in ancient times. Reared as a beast of burden, he is used also as a source of wool and meat.

(above) A herd of sheep grazing on the island of Texel in the extreme north of Holland. A green cheese famous in the north is made from their milk. (below, left) A herd of camels. (right) A majestic Mehari. The difference between the camel and dromedary is small. Both are able to live in extremely dry climates; both have one or two humps, which they use to store water. Both have a rubbery cushion under their feet, which allows them to walk over sand and rough ground. What's different is the coats of each animal. The dromedary's fur is not as thick or as wooly as the camel's, because he lives in a warm climate.

A picture of the water buck, so called because they avoid forests to live in the open plains near streams and rivers. They are shy and very fast, their long legs able to carry them at dazzling speed.

Here I am again, boys and girls. Never have a few moments of separation seemed so long! It was quite a ride, too. Now I'd like to tell you something: the real forefather of our saddle and cart horses was the equus Prezwalski—that is, the horse (equus is the Latin word for horse) discovered by the Russian explorer Nikolaj Michailovic Prezwalski while traveling in Mongolia. This horse was called *kertag* or *kortag* and lived in "the country of animals," the Mongolian name for that part of their country.

What a shame it would have been not to be able to trace back to the forefather of one of man's closest friends. And so once more we must let man pay his due to his four-legged friend. Nature, that incredibly marvelous force, is generous to those who love her creatures large and small.

THE END OF THE JOURNEY—FOR NOW

I believe that you, my friends, have enjoyed this very swift gallop through the world of mammals as much as I have. I might even say we've found it an exalting experience.

You and I together have met the animals in their own environment and learned something about them. In order for the meeting between us and the animals to take place, we had to be moved by a feeling of love for all the creatures which live in our world. I know that you have this love in your hearts, because you've been the best traveling companions anyone could ask for.

Your Donald, one who knows he has your love,

With affection,

left no record of having horses before 1800 B.C. The Egyptians first used this animal in 1675 B.C. On the other hand, the wild donkey *was* utilized by the Sumerians to pull their chariots of war. Our modern domestic donkey originated from the wild African donkey, already tamed around 3200 B.C. in the Nile valley, and later put to use in Mesopotamia and Palestine. But the Asian wild donkey cannot be considered the forefather of the animal we know today.

The camel, with two humps, was already domesticated 1000 years before Christ, in Persia. But we know almost nothing about the history of the African and Arabian dromedary.

122

INDEX